P9-DUR-992

José Roleo Santiago
A world traveller who has covered three-quarters of the world for over a quarter of a century. José is also the author of Lonely Planet's *Pakistan - a travel survival kit*.

THANK YOU
For information supplied by:

Patrick Barbay (F), David Clarke (Canada), Patrick Doran (UK), Melvin Duddridge (UK), Tom Eggert (USA), Tom Harriman & Jan King (USA), Ronald Heinsath (Can), Stewart Henderson & Mary Barrett (Aus), Mark Dwyer (Aus), Christopher Hoeth (CH), Marco Keiner & Hubert Lohr (D), Adrian Peter King (Aus), John Ormonde (Ire), P Pomarede (Can), Hans Ritsch (D), Elizabeth Seifert (D), Maung Tin (Bur), Judith Tregear & David Murray-Smith (Aus), Gregory Wait (Aus), Harald Weber (NL), Kathryn Wells & Gary Anderson (Aus), Rick Wicks (USA)

Aus – Australia, Bur – Burma, Can – Canada, CH – Switzerland, D – West Germany, F – France, NL – Netherlands, UK – UK, USA – USA

.... and to the kindly people of Bangladesh and the staff of the Parjatan Tourism Corporation for making it possible to complete this book.

AND A REQUEST
Things change – prices go up, good places go bad, bad places go out of business, new places appear, new possibilities are tried out. If you find things better, worse or just different please write and tell us. We love getting those letters from 'our travellers' out on the road and, as usual, we'll reward good letters with a free copy of the next edition of this book or of another Lonely Planet guidebook.

Contents

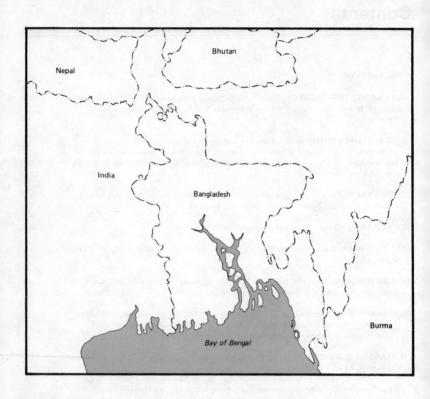

Introduction

The existence of Bangladesh is known to the world principally via the adage that 'the only good news is bad news'. Floods, famine and less than democratic changes in government seems to be the extent of the interest that the world can show in this small nation. Combine this with the overpowering proximity of India and it is hardly surprising that Bangladesh doesn't rate highly on the itinerary of most travellers through Asia. What this image doesn't reveal, however, is that Bangladesh, despite its problems, offers a variety of attractions quite unique for a country its size.

Nestled in the crook of the Bay of Bengal and braided by the fingers of the Ganges delta, Bangladesh offers the adventurous traveller verdant tropical forests, one of the longest (and widest) shark-free beaches in the world, national parks so dense they are only accessible by boat, and the remnants of colonial cultures dating back to the Moghul Empire.

Divided into four administrative divisions, travel is easy and quick, with only short distances to be covered to reach markedly different environments. And for those who prefer to move at a more leisurely pace the countless rivers make water travel the norm rather than the exception.

In the east there are the lush tea-growing hills of Sylhet, and gracious Sylhet town itself, while in the south, around Cox's Bazar and Chittagong, tropical forests and long beaches stretching down into Burma regularly attract thousands. The west and north are riverine plains, dotted with thousands of ruined temples and palaces still lying abandoned in the fields. In the centre of the country, just below the junction of the two major rivers of the subcontinent, the Ganges and the Brahmaputra, is Dacca, capital of the nation. The history of the Old City, established by the original Moghul settlers, the grand edifices built during British rule, and many peaceful parks and gardens make this a highlight in any visit.

Bangladesh makes no attempt to compete with India. Though connected by history this nation is proud of its hard won independence and is working towards a more stable footing. The National Tourist Corporation's slogan acknowledges its countries perceived limitations, but like them you could do worse than use it to your advantage – come to Bangladesh before the tourists.

Facts about the Country

HISTORY

The history of Bangladesh has been one of extremes; of turmoil and peace, prosperity and destitution. It has thrived under the glow of cultural splendour and suffered under the ravages of war.

Stretching from the lower reaches of the Ganges River on the Bay of Bengal and north almost to the foothills of the Himalaya, this region of the subcontinent is the gateway to Burma and the Far East, making control over it vital to successive Indian empires. The strategic position of the Bengal area has ensured its place in the political, cultural and religious conflicts and developments of the subcontinent through the millennia.

Throughout its tumultuous history it has known internal warfare, suffered invasion upon invasion, witnessed the rise and fall of mighty empires, benefited from the trade and culture brought from foreign lands, and been both blessed and cursed by the introduction of new religions.

Early History

The history of Bengal is relatively obscure until the 3rd century BC when it was part of the extensive Mauryan empire inherited by the Emperor Ashoka. Perhaps the earliest mention of the region is in the Hindu epic the *Mahabharata* (the Great Battle – 9th century BC) which tells of Prince Bhima's conquest of eastern India, including Varendra, an ancient kingdom in what is now Bangladesh.

In the 5th and 6th centuries BC, as Aryan influence spread eastward from its original foothold on the Indus (in Pakistan), most of northern India became united culturally but remained politically at odds. Warfare between these northern states finally resulted in the formation of the single kingdom of Magadha with its capital at Patna on the Ganges.

In 325 BC, a young adventurer called Chandragupta Maurya seized the Magadhan throne and laid the foundation for an empire which eventually spread right across northern India. It reached its peak under his grandson, the Emperor Ashoka, one of the classic figures of Indian history. Ashoka's conversion to Buddhism in 262 BC had a long lasting effect on the religious life of the area. Even as late as the 7th century AD Chinese pilgrims still found Buddhism prevalent in Bengal, though already in fierce conflict with Hinduism.

The Mauryan empire, under Ashoka, controlled more of India than any subsequent ruler prior to the British. Following his death the empire went into a rapid decline and finally collapsed in 184 BC. It was not until the 4th century AD that northern India was once again united under imperial rule, this time by the Guptas, during whose reign the arts flourished and Buddhism reached its zenith.

The Guptas succumbed to a fresh wave of White Hun invasions and in the 6th century AD Sasanaka founded the Ganda empire in Bengal. This was overthrown by the warrior-king Sri Harsa who ruled until the 8th century AD when anarchy and chaos finally toppled the empire. Buddhism was in decline and Hinduism was experiencing a resurgence and over the next couple of centuries while northern India broke into a number of separate kingdoms the Bengal area established a separate political identity.

Internal conflicts continued until Gopala, a tribal chief, emerged as an elected leader and became the founding figure of the Pala dynasty (8th to 12th century AD). The Palas were Buddhists who claimed to have descended from the sea and the sun. They continued their royal patronage of Buddhism while politically tolerating the Hindus.

In 805 AD, after the death of Devapal, the Pala dynasty was considerably weakened but gained momentum again in the 10th century under Mahapala I when the empire enjoyed a period of prosperity. It did not last long, however, as its very prosperity brought a succession of invasions from the east, west and south. It was the Hindu Senas from South India who were eventually to replace the Palas as rulers in Bengal. But in less than a century both Palas and Senas, Buddhists and Hindus, were swamped by the flood of Muslim invaders and the tide of Islam.

The Muslim Period

Muslim power had been creeping towards India from the Middle East for centuries before Mohammed Bakhtiar, a Khiljis from the Turkestan region of Central Asia, appeared on the scene. With only 20 men and a remarkable bluff, Bakhtiar captured Bengal in 1199 and brought the area under the rule of the Sultanate of Delhi, the centre of Muslim power which already held sway over most of northern India.

For a short period the Mameluk Sultanate was established in Bengal, but in the 14th century this was overrun by the hordes of Tamerlane, and the Tughluk Sultanate was formed. The influx of Muslims from Samarkand, Balkh and Abyssinia, and of Persians from Shiraz continued and under the Muslims Bengal entered a new era. Cities developed; palaces sprung up along with forts, mosques, mausoleums and gardens; roads and bridges were constructed; and prosperity brought a new cultural life.

The Afghans arrived in 1520 and contributed further to the urbanisation of the land. The city of Gaur in particular emerged as a cosmopolitan metropolis.

In 1526 the Sultanate of Delhi was overthrown by Babur, a descendant of both Timur and Genghis Khan, and the Moghul Empire under this Central Asian leader reached out to encompass most of northern India. It was not until 1576,

however, that the Moghuls managed to take control of Bengal. Babur's grandson Akbar finally defeated Sultan Daud Karrani at the Battle of Tukaroi and Bengal became a *subha* (province) of the Moghul Empire.

Gaur remained the centre of power in Bengal until the capital was moved to Dacca in 1608 and under the Moghul viceroys urbanisation continued, art and literature flourished, overland trade expanded and Bengal was opened to the world maritime trade. Intellectual and cultural life at this time was influenced mainly by the Persians, particularly by the *sufis*, Muslim mystics who spoke in verses and wrote poetry.

Glorious at its peak the Moghul Empire ushered in another golden age in India, only to be outdone by the country's final great colonial power – the British.

European Period

The fate of Moghul rule in Bengal was decided long before its final decline became apparent in the 18th century. With the coming of international maritime trade and commerce, Europeans began to establish themselves in the region. The Portuguese had founded settlements as early as the 15th century, and were soon joined by the East India Company – a London-based trading firm that had been granted a royal charter by Queen Elizabeth I in 1600, giving them a monopoly over British trade with India.

After a few initial setbacks – the Portuguese were ousted from their foothold in 1633 by Bengali opposition, while the British failed in an attempt to capture Chittagong in 1686 – the European juggernaut was unstoppable. The British managed to negotiate trade terms with the authorities in Bengal, and established a fortified trading post at Calcutta, dealing mainly in cotton, raw silk, yarn, sugar and saltpetre.

Following the death of Aurangzeb in 1707 came the decline of Moghul power, and the provincial governors of the once

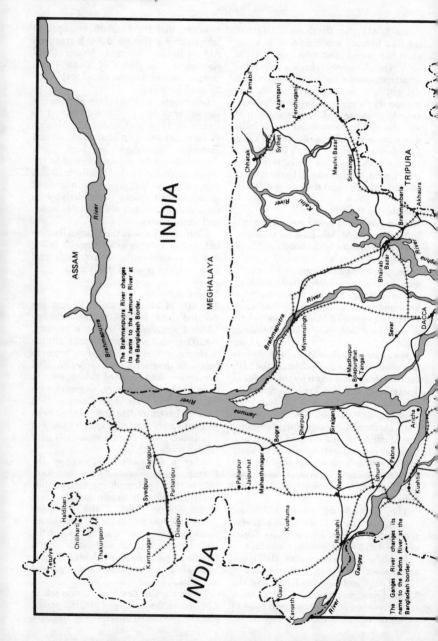

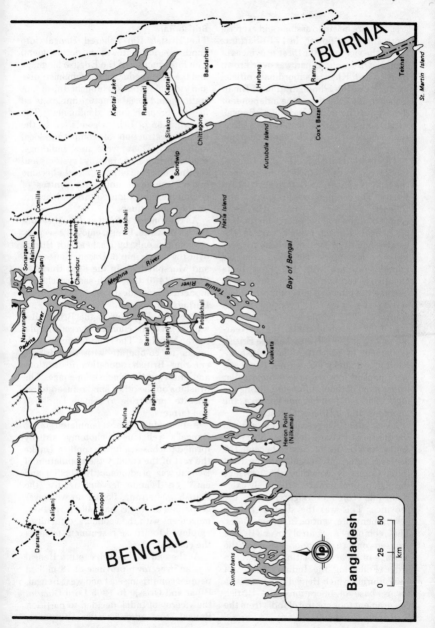

great empire began to assume and exercise more and more power. In 1740 Sarfaraz Khan, the viceroy of the three provinces of Bengal, Orissa and Bihar, was overthrown by Ali Vardi Khan, a subordinate official in charge of the administration of Bihar. This heralded the rise of the independent dynasty of the nawab-nazims of Bengal, with whom the Englishman Robert Clive, then a clerk with the East India Company, came in contact.

The initial British foothold in Bengal, the East India Company's trading post on the Hooghly River, was a thriving concern by now. The company was prosperous and Calcutta was fast becoming the great centre of trade and commerce on the Bay of Bengal. Robert Clive's part in the establishment of British hegemony over India is legendary. He rose from his humble position with the East India Company, through military success, to become the effective governor of Bengal, setting the stage for eventual British control over the whole country.

In 1756 Suraj-ud-daula, the 21-year-old nawab of Bengal, attacked the British settlement of Calcutta. The British inhabitants unlucky enough not to escape were packed into an underground cellar where most of them suffocated during the night. This incident became known as the infamous 'Black Hole of Calcutta'.

A year later Clive retook Calcutta and in the Battle of Plassey defeated Suraj-ud-daula. As a result the British became the de facto rulers of Bengal and the East India Company governed the province through puppet nawabs, effectively exercising its *raj* (sovereignty) over the province. This was the start of British government intervention in Indian affairs. The company's control over Bengal aroused concern in London, leading to the passage of an act regulating its power in India. Following the Indian Mutiny of 1857, during which Bengal was used as a secure base of operations, the British Government took control of India from the East India Company.

British Raj

The British Raj ushered Bengal into another period of growth and development. The introduction of the English language and the British educational, administrative and judicial systems established an organizational and social structure unparalleled in its breadth and dominance. The introduction of British goods led to the virtual destruction of competing local industries. There were new buildings, roads, bridges, a railway system and continued urbanisation. Calcutta became one of the most important centres of commerce, education, culture and the arts on the subcontinent.

As the longest settled and most secure British province, Bengal enjoyed a security interrupted only by clashes with Burma over the ownership of Dacca, Chittagong and Murshidabad. In the First Burmese War (1824-6) the south-eastern claw of modern Bangladesh was saved from Burmese annexation.

The establishment of the British Raj was a relief to the Hindus but a catastrophe for the Muslims. The Hindus immediately began to co-operate with the British, entering British education institutions and studying the English language. The Muslims on the other hand refused to co-operate, preferring to remain landlords and farmers.

As one of India's most populated states, Bengal's religious dichotomy already formed the basis of future conflict. Unlike the rest of the country the population of Bengal was predominantly Muslim and early on Islamic fervour against the British was strong, flaring up whenever crops failed. It was basically a religious movement with the economic difficulties employed to arouse resentment towards the colonial rulers.

At the end of the 19th century Bengal was an overgrown province of 78 million people, comprising east and west Bengal, Bihar and Orissa. In 1905 Lord Curzon, the viceroy of India, decided to partition Bengal for administrative purposes, creating a new province of East Bengal and Assam with 31 million people and its capital at Dacca.

The Indian National Congress, which had been formed in 1885, was originally supported by both Hindus and Muslims. But the division of Bengal was seen as a religious partition, prompting the formation of the All India Muslim League in the following year. Its purpose was the protection of Muslim interests, as the Congress was increasingly perceived as becoming a Hindu power group.

This first partition of Bengal was physically defined by the Brahmaputra and the Padma rivers. East Bengal prospered, Dacca assumed its old status as capital and Chittagong became an important sea port.

Although the partition of Bengal was opposed by Hindus and Muslims alike, when the split province was reunited in 1912 the Muslims began to have doubts. They feared Hindu social, economic and even political dominance and continued to press for Muslim autonomy.

At the same time the imperial capital of the British Raj was moved to Delhi and although Calcutta remained an important commercial, cultural and political centre the rest of Bengal was neglected. Political agitation increased over the next few decades as did the violent enmity between Muslims and Hindus. Although there was a movement in favour of a united Bengal the Muslims supported repartition and the formation of a Muslim home state separate from India.

Independence

As the Indian National Congress continued to press for self rule for India, the British began to map out a path to independence. At the close of WW II it was clear that European colonialism had run its course and Indian independence was inevitable. Moreover, Britain no longer had the desire or power to maintain its vast empire, and a major problem had developed within India itself.

The large Muslim minority realised that an independent India would be a nation dominated by Hindus and that despite Mahatma Gandhi's fair-minded and even-handed approach, others in the Indian National Congress would not be so accommodating or tolerant. The country was divided on purely religious grounds with the Muslim League headed by Muhammad Ali Jinnah, representing the majority of Muslims, and the Indian Congress Party, led by Jawaharlal Nehru, commanding the Hindu population.

India achieved independence in 1947 but the struggle after the war had been bitter, especially in Bengal where the fight for self-government was complicated by the conflict between Hindus and Muslims. The British realised any agreement between the Muslim League and the Indian National Congress was impossible so the viceroy, Lord Mountbatten, seeing no other option, decided to partition the subcontinent.

East Pakistan

Once the decision was made the most difficult and important step was deciding the actual location for the new state. The two overwhelmingly Muslim regions were on the exact opposite sides of the subcontinent, in Bengal and the Punjab. In Bengal, Calcutta, with its Hindu majority, its jute mills and its port facilities contrasted invidiously with Muslim-dominated East Bengal, also a major jute producer, but without any manufacturing or port facilities.

The Muslim League's demand for an independent Muslim home state carved out of India yet separate from it, was realised in 1947 with the creation of Pakistan. This was uniquely achieved by establishing it in two separate states, East and West, on either side of the country and divided by 1600 km of hostile Hindu Indian territory. For months the greatest exodus in human history took place as Hindus moved to India and Muslims moved to East or West Pakistan.

But despite the fact that support for the creation of Pakistan was based on Islamic solidarity and a desire to end Hindu dominance the two halves of the new state had little else in common. The instability of the arrangement was self-evident, not only in the geographical sense, but for economic, political and social reasons as well.

The people of East Pakistan spoke only Bengali while the West Pakistanis spoke Urdu, Pushtu, Punjabi and Sindhi; the diet of the East consisted mainly of fish and rice while the Westerners ate meat and wheat. There were even ethnic differences; the long Aryan influence had produced a taller, lighter-skinned people in West Pakistan.

The country was administered from West Pakistan which tended to monopolise aid money and other revenues even though it was East Pakistan that had the bulk of the population and produced most of the cash crops. Early on these differences and inequalities stirred up a sense of Bengali nationalism that had not been reckoned with in the struggle for Muslim independence.

The Bengalis of East Pakistan had no desire to play a subordinate role to the West Pakistanis in defence, administration, economic and foreign affairs. The resentment was exacerbated by the fact that when the British left, all the Hindus in the administrative service fled en masse to India, leaving a vacuum that could only be filled by the trained West Pakistanis and not by the local Muslims. Trade, the services and commercial and banking enterprises were likewise controlled by the West. There was dissatisfaction in all spheres of Bengali life.

When Mohammad Ali Jinnah and the Pakistan Government declared that 'Urdu and only Urdu' would be the national language the Bengalis decided it was time to assert their cultural identity. The primacy given to Urdu resulted in the Bengali language movement which rapidly became a Bengali national movement.

There were riots in Dacca in 1952 during which 12 students were killed by the Pakistan army. Democracy gave way to military government and martial law.

The Language Movement, led by Sheikh Mujibur Rahman, emerged as the national political party in East Pakistan, and became the ideological underpinning for the Awami League in its drive for internal self-government.

Under pressure Pakistan's President Yahya Khan held elections in 1971 in which the Awami League won 167 of the 313 seats in the National Assembly, a clear majority over the People's Progressive Party led by Zulfikhar Ali Bhutto. Constitutionally the Awami League should have formed the government of Pakistan, but the President, faced with this unacceptable result, postponed the opening of the assembly.

Riots and strikes broke out in East Pakistan and tension increased as the troubles took greater toll of lives. At Chittagong a clash between civilians and soldiers left 55 Bengalis dead. When President Khan secretly returned to West Pakistan after talks with Sheikh Mujib in March 1971, Pakistan troops took to the streets killing, looting and burning.

The Bangladesh War
Sheikh Mujib declared East Pakistan to be the independent state of Bangladesh – land of the Bangala speakers. He was arrested, taken to West Pakistan and thrown in jail. This ignited the smouldering rebellion in the east wing and when the Mukti Bahini – the Bangladesh freedom fighters – captured the Chittagong radio station, Ziaur Rahman announced the birth of the new country and called upon its people to resist at all costs.

President Khan responded by sending more than a thousand troops to quell the rebellion and the ensuing war was one of the shortest but bloodiest of modern times. Yahya Khan was determined to rid the country of Sheikh Mujib's supporters. In carrying out this task, his troops began the systematic slaughter of the Mukti Bahini and other 'subversive' elements such as intellectuals and Hindus.

With only captured guns and primitive weapons at their disposal the freedom fighters were at a serious disadvantage until Indian arms came to the aid of the Mukti Bahini, who were soon organised throughout the country.

Pakistan took Dacca and secured other major cities, and by November 1971 the whole country suffered the chilling burden of the Pakistani army. The searches, looting, rape and slaughter of civilians continued and in the nine months from the end of March 1971, 10 million people had fled to refugee camps in India.

Border clashes between Pakistan and India became more frequent as the Mukti Bahini, who were being trained and equipped by India, were using the border as a pressure valve against the Pakistani onslaught. But when the Pakistan Air Force led a pre-emptive air attack on Indian forces on 3 December 1971 it was open warfare and the end came quickly. Indian troops crossed the Bengal border, liberated Jessore on 7 December and prepared to take Dacca. The occupying army of West Pakistan was being attacked from the west by the Indian army, from the north and east by the Mukti Bahini and from all quarters by the civilian population.

By 14 December the Indian victory was complete and the Pakistani forces surrendered to the Indian army. Pakistan's General Niazi signed the surrender agreement on 16 December. On his release from jail, Sheikh Mujib took over the reins of government. He announced the establishment of the world's 139th country – Bangladesh was born.

Bangladesh

The People's Republic of Bangladesh was a country born into chaos; shattered by war, with a ruined economy and a totally disrupted communication system the country seemed fated to continuing disaster. Pakistan's pogrom against intel-

lectuals had decimated the new country's educated class and it appeared that Sheikh Mujib, though a skillful leader in wartime, did not have the peacetime ability to heal the wounds.

The famine of 1973-4 set the war-ravaged land and its people back even more. A state of emergency was declared in 1974 and Sheikh Mujib proclaimed himself President. The abuses and corrupt practices of politicians and their relatives, however, prompted a military coup in 1975, during which Sheikh Mujib Rahman and his houshold were slaughtered.

Khandakar Mushtaq Ahmed became President, declared martial law and banned all political activities. A counter-coup four months later brought Brigadier Khalid Musharaf into power – for four days. He was overthrown and killed, and power was assumed by a military triumvirate led by Abusadet Mohammed Sayem, the Chief Justice of the Supreme Court. Justice Sayem, as President and Chief Martial Law Administrator, governed for nearly two years, with the heads of the armed services as his deputies.

In November 1976 the head of the army staff, General Ziaur Rahman, who had led the Mukti Bahini during the War of Independence, took over as Chief Martial Law Administrator and, following the resignation of President Sayem in April 1977, assumed the presidency.

The overwhelming victory of President Zia (as Ziaur Rahman was popularly known) in the 1978 presidential poll was further consolidated when his newly formed Bangladesh Nationalist Party won two-thirds of the seats in the parliamentary elections of 1979. Democracy returned to Bangladesh in 1979 when martial law was lifted and under Zia, who proved to be a competent politician and statesman, Bangladesh achieved a degree of stability. As he turned more and more to the west and the oil-rich Islamic countries, assistance began pouring into the troubled state and over the next five years the economy went from strength to strength.

During an attempted coup on 30 May 1981 President Ziaur Rahman was assassinated by a group of military men led by Major-General Mohammed Abdul Manzur. There was no obvious successor to Zia but Justice Abdus Sattar was appointed as acting-president. Faced with population in a political frenzy a general election was held in which Sattar, as candidate for the BNP, won 66% of the vote. He formed a cabinet and the country appeared ready to settle down. The population's peaceful return to the rule of the law following the attempted coup and resulting election was a reflection of the stability Ziaur Rahman had created.

However there was increasing concern over government methods and on 24 March 1982 General Hossain Mohammed Ershad seized power in a bloodless coup and once again Bangladesh was placed under martial law. Ershad announced a mixed cabinet of politicians, army officers and diplomats, and pledged a return to parliamentary rule within two years.

This pledge, however, has yet to be honoured, and it seems less and less likely that it will. The habit of power and a liking for the fruits that it brings have recently put Bangladesh further away from any form of popularly elected government. The general election scheduled for 6 April 1985 was not held. In its place Ershad held a referendum in an attempt to pacify some of his more vehement critics. The question 'do you support the policies and programmes of Ershad and agree that he should remain in power until elections are held' received a 75% response of which 94% were, according to Ershad, in his favour. The opposition parties dismissed this as a farce, and claimed that the 75% turnout was actually only 50% in reality.

Despite his apparent disregard for both pledge and the spirit of democracy, Ershad is acknowledged by some to have done a capable job in managing the economy.

Chronology of Events Leading to Independence

1947 The contiguous Muslim majority parts of the British Indian provinces of Bengal and Assam are carved out to form the province of East Bengal, which is united with the geographically separated Muslim provinces of the north-western part of British India in a federal Muslim state called Pakistan.

1954 The United Front of the opposition parties, demanding maximum regional autonomy for East Bengal among other things, defeats the ruling Muslim league by capturing 97% of the seats in the first elections to the provincial legislature. The United Front Government is dismissed within weeks of assuming power by the Central Pakistan Government on the pretext of anti-national attitudes.

1956 The first Constitution of Pakistan is adopted, forming a highly centralised federation between East Bengal (renamed East Pakistan) and the provinces of West Pakistan (soon afterwards unified into one province). East Pakistan is given fewer representatives per head of electorate in the National Assembly than West Pakistan.

1958 Scheduled national elections are cancelled. General Ayub Khan takes power through a military coup and imposes a virtually unitary form of government giving the authoritarian Central Government the power to appoint and dismiss the Provincial Government, which was not responsible to the legislature elected on the basis of very limited franchise.

1966 Sheikh Mujibur Rahman of the Awami League demands the autonomy of East Pakistan on the basis of a six-point programme which envisaged a central government with responsibilities for defence and foreign affairs only while giving all taxation and economic powers to the provincial governments.

1968 The Pakistan Government attempts to crush the autonomy movement by instituting a conspiracy trial against Sheikh Mujib and others.

1969 A nationwide political upsurge topples Ayub Khan, who is succeeded by General Yahya Khan. The latter promises elections to transfer power to the popular representatives.

1970 The Sheikh's Awami League wins a massive electoral victory in December, capturing all but two seats in the National Assembly from East Pakistan.

1971 On 25-26 March the Pakistan army cracks down on the autonomist forces who were demanding immediate transfer of power to the elected party in East Pakistan on the basis of complete regional autonomy. Mass killing and destruction in Dacca and elsewhere in East Pakistan follow the arrest of the Sheikh by the army. The Government of the People's Republic of Bangladesh is proclaimed in April by the nationalist resistance led by the Awami League and spearheaded by the rebellious Bengalis in the Pakistan army. India provides sanctuary to Bangladesh guerrillas. Tension builds up between India and Pakistan leading to the outbreak of full-scale war in early December. The joint Indian and Bangladesh Command accepts the surrender of the Pakistan army in Dacca on 16 December.

1972 Bangladesh is recognised by most European and Asian countries by February. Indian army withdrawal from Bangladesh completed on 12 March.

Note on Nomenclature
'Bangala' or 'Bangla' is the traditional local-language name of the linguistic area consisting of the present state of Bangladesh and the present Indian state of West Bengal.

POPULATION & PEOPLE
The population of Bangladesh is approaching the 100 million mark, making it the most densely populated country in the world. There are 1656 people per square km, with the highest density of population (about 700 per square km) in the areas of the Lower Padma and the Meghna rivers.

The Chittagong district in the south-east has the lowest density, with about 40 people per square km.

The 1975 population growth rate of 3.4% was reduced to 2.7% in 1982 but still exceeded the economic growth rate for the same year. Only 5% of the population constitute the top consumers; 80% live below the poverty line; and the remainder live in abject conditions. The illiteracy rate in Bangladesh is more than 80%.

People
Bangladesh, like most recently established nations, is a mixture of people of varied origins, in this case a melting pot of the Dravidian, Aryan and Tibeto-Burmese racial stocks. Over the centuries immigrants and invaders from India, Afghanistan, Persia, Iraq and Saudi Arabia have endowed the country with an ethnic diversity that can be seen most obviously in the varying skin colours.

The Dravidians, with their racial origins in the Deccan Plateau, are mainly Hindus and constitute about 14% of the population. The Muslims who make up more than 80% are of Dravido-Aryan stock. The original tribal people still exist, mainly in the Chittagong Hill Tracts, though they now number less than 1% of the total population. The Tibeto-Burmese inhabitants are mainly Buddhists and less than 1% of the population are Christians.

The Muslims and Hindus have a cultural affinity with West Bengal and speak Bengali, while the Buddhists have their own distinct culture and dialects related mainly to that of Burma and the tribal culture of eastern India. The tiny Christian population here mostly have Portuguese names and are usually English-speakers.

There are about half a million Muslim Biharis in Bangladesh, some of them living in refugee camps in Dacca waiting approval to live in Pakistan. Owing to population pressure on the plains many tribal hill folk have fled into north-east India and are a major cause of the continuing instability in that part of India.

Tribal People

The tribal population of Bangladesh numbers almost one million. They live generally in the hilly regions north of Mymensingh, the district of Sylhet, and more than half a million are concentrated in the wooded Chittagong Hill Tracts. Others now live in urban areas such as Chittagong and Cox's Bazar.

The tribes living in the hill tracts of Chittagong include the Chakmas, Moghs, Mrus, Murangs, Lushais, Kukis, Bams, Tripuras, Saks, Tangchangyas, Shandus, Banjugis and the Pankhars. The Chakmas constitute the major tribe here and next to them are the Moghs, who are also found in Cox's Bazar and the Khepupara region of the Patuakhali district.

The tribes in the Sylhet Hills – the Kharsis, Pangous and the Manipuris – usually have their settlements on the hilly frontier area at the foot of the Khasia-Jayantia Hills. Some of them have become businessmen and jewellers in Sylhet.

The Garos, Hanjongis, Hadis, Dahuis, Palais and the Bunas live in the hilly regions north of Mymensingh in Haluaghat, Sreebardi, Kalmakanda and the Garo Hills and some are located in the forest-clad highlands of Madhupur in the Tangail district.

Other tribal groups, such as the Santals, Oraons, Hus, Mundus and Rajbansis are scattered in urban settlements in Rangpur, Dinajpur, Bogra, Rajshahi, Noakhali, Comilla and Bakerganj.

The tribes in the Mymensingh Hills were originally nomads from the eastern states of India and those in the Chittagong Hill Tracts originate from Burma. The tribal groups have their own distinct culture, art, religious beliefs, superstitions, farming methods and attire. Many of the tribes are Buddhist though some still retain their animist religion which, to some extent, have been influenced by Hinduism. Cannibalism and the offering

Chakma Tribal Woman Spinning

of human sacrifices, once part of the ritual of some tribes who believed that slaying another man endowed the slayer with the victim's attributes, is now happily a thing of the past.

Rice and wine are the staple food of these hill people, but included in the tribal menu – now minus the humans – are snakes, beetles, crabs, fish, snails, pigs, dogs, buffaloes, deer, ants and chickens. Many of the tribes influenced by Hinduism, along with the Chakmas, Moghs and Marmas who are Buddhist, cremate their dead. Others, like the Kharsis, bury their dead and place headstones on their graves. Their attire is minimal, apparently because their beliefs enjoin them to wear little clothing. Some have begun to wear more clothing, but always leaving the left shoulder exposed as a sign of submission to the *Turai* – the creator.

Their dwellings are usually grass huts, either on stilts or flat on the ground and the farming methods are primitive. Some still retain curious traditional customs or rites such as the stone-lifting ceremony of the Kharsis, which must have originated from Tibet or even the northern mountain areas of Pakistan.

Many of the tribes still have very little contact with the outside world, but as modern civilisation begins to encroach on their territories more and more of the younger villagers are moving to the urban areas for employment. The Chakmas, for instance, now make saris and tribal jewellery and have established or joined weaving industries. They have begun to accept education, more clothing and even use modern medicine in lieu of herbs and mantras.

ECONOMY

Officially Bangladesh is the second poorest nation in the world after Bhutan. At last count there were over 80 voluntary aid agencies, besides the many official and semi-official aid agencies like the UNO, UNICEF, UNDP, UNESCO, WHO, USAID, operating in Bangladesh. Economically, Bangladesh is most renowned for its poverty rather than any saleable product, industry or resource. Foreign aid provides nearly 90% of the country's development budget.

Historically, the region of Bengal was known for its production of jute, the 'golden fibre', in the last century. This remains one of its principal cash crops alongside tea, timber and fish.

Internally, the economy functions only at an agrarian subsistence level for 80% of the people, and with such a level of poverty there is very little chance of any expansion through primary production. The soil is incredibly fertile, but virtually every scrap of land which could be used for agricultural purposes already is. Improvements in food production can only come through improved technology – fertilizers, irrigation, multiple-cropping. Yet 40% of farmers do not have farm animals or even ploughs. Bangladesh is a net importer of foodstuffs, mainly rice and wheat.

Any attempt to set Bangladesh's economy to rights seems faced with insurmountable obstructions: Bangladesh is ravaged regularly by cyclones which inundate large portions of the arable land; it is vastly over-populated; it is short of important natural resource; what little economic infrastructure it had was destroyed during the 1971 war of liberation; land-yields are extremely low, production is approximately a quarter of that produced per hectare in Australian.

Countries like Bangladesh give a new meaning to the term 'third world'. As a country it has been described, in terms of aid, as a 'bottomless basket'; to compare it with fellow third-world states, like the oil-rich Arab countries or even neighbouring Burma is ludicrous. Bangladesh is not a third world state, it is a fourth if not fifth world state.

Government Policy

With nationhood, the government pursued a socialist economic policy, nationalising

80% of the economy, including banks, major corporations and industries. From 1977, the policy was changed whereby foreign companies were compensated for nationalized assets on condition they re-invest in the country. In general, all nationalized bodies were returned to their former owners. Since then, there has been a nominal statistical improvement in the economy.

GEOGRAPHY

Bangladesh has a total area of 143,998 square km, roughly the same size as England and Wales. It is surrounded to the west, north-west and east by India, and shares a south-eastern border with Burma for 283 km. To the south is the Bay of Bengal.

The topography is characterized by alluvial plains, bounded to the north by the submontane regions of the Himalaya; the piedmontane areas in the north-east and the eastern fringes adjacent to Assam, Tripura and Burma are broken by the forested hills of Mymensingh, Sylhet, and Chittagong. The great Himalayan rivers, the Ganges and the Brahmaputra, divide the land into four major regions: north-west, south-west, central and eastern.

The Ganges, which begins in the Indian state of Uttar Pradesh, enters Bangladesh from the north-west through the division of Rajshahi. It joins the Brahmaputra in the centre of the country, north of the capital, Dacca. At this stage many tributaries have formed, all heading southwards to drain out into the Bay of Bengal. But the Ganges and the Brahmaputra rivers both receive new names once they pass into Bangladesh: the Ganges becomes the Padma, while the Brahmaputra is known as the Jamuna. It is these great rivers and the countless tributaries that flow from them that have the most apparent effect on the landform: constant erosion and flooding over the alluvial plains change the course of rivers, landscapes, and agriculture. The Jamuna alone is estimated to carry down 900 million tons of silt each year.

The alluvial river plains, which dominate nine-tenths of the country, are very flat and never rise more than 10 metres above sea level. The only relief from these alluvial plains occurs in the north-east and south-east corners of the country where the hills rise to an average of 240 metres and 600 metres respectively. These hills follow a north-south direction. The highest peak in Bangladesh is Keokradong at 1230 metres.

Overall, Bangladesh has no great mountains or deserts, is more characterized by wooded marshlands and jungles, with forest regions in Sylhet, Mymensingh, Sundarbans and the Chittagong Hill Tracts and Tangail in the Dacca division. These forest regions constitute 15% of the total land area.

Almost all of Bangladesh's coastline forms the mouths of the Ganges, the final destination of the Ganges and the largest estuarine delta in the world. The coastal strip from the western border to Chitt-agong is one great patchwork of shifting river courses and little islands. Over the whole delta area, which extends into India, the rivers make up 6.5% of the total area.

The south-eastern coast, south from the city of Chittagong, is backed by the wooded Arakan Hill chain which overlooks a sandy coast for about 120 km through to the settlement of Teknaf on the southern-most point.

FESTIVALS & HOLIDAYS

A festival in Bangladesh – as in Pakistan, India and Nepal – is usually called a *mela*. Though a Muslim state, melas in Bang-ladesh are often a time when all religious sects – Buddhists, Christians and Hindus – join in the celebrations; melas could be likened to a spectator sport, but one where everybody joins in despite their allegiances. Festivals may be related to harvests and other religious rites and ceremonies of the Hindus and Buddhists.

Minor melas are mainly related to weddings, exhibition fairs or even election victories.

Hindu Festivals
Festival of the Bera This is a Hindu boat festival held on the rivers between August and September. The Bera is an effigy made of paper resembling a falcon, but with the breast and crest of a peacock. This is all placed on a raft made of plantains (bananas), set on fire and set sail down a river.

Holi Fest The festival of colours is celebrated in the first week of March in Bangladesh.

Jagannath Festival In Dhamrai, 32 km north of Dacca, on the banks of the Bangshi River, a big mela is held every year. The main attraction is the gigantic chariot of the Hindu god Jagannath which is dragged through the streets.

Islamic Festivals
Muslim festivals follow the Lunar Calendar, which comes 10 days earlier than the western calendar each year. Hindu and Buddhist holidays also follow a different calendar but they generally fall at much the same date each year.

Shab-e-Barat
  Sacred night when alms and sweets are distributed to the poor.
Jamat-ul-Wida
  Start of the month of Ramadan and the fasting period.
Id-ul-Fitri
  Celebrates the day the Koran was revealed to the Prophet; celebrated with the end of Ramadan.
Id-ul-Azha
  Sacrifice of Ismail, celebrated with the slaughter of sheep and goats for distribution to the poor; pilgrimage to Mecca begins.
Moharram (Azhura)
  Martyrdom of Imman Hussain in Karbala.

Id-e-Milad-un-Nabi
  Birth of the Prophet Mohammed.
Ramadan
  The month of the Koran's revelation; a month of fasting from dawn to dusk. Though religiously observed, food stores and restaurants in the main cities tend to stay open during Ramadan.

National Holidays
21 February Ekushey Day – day when several students were killed from the Language Movement.
26 March Independence Day
1 May Labour Day
30 June Bank Holiday
7 November National Revolution Day
16 December Biganj Dibash – Liberation Day
25 December Christmas
31 December Bank Holiday

CULTURE
Apart from its religious distinction Bangladesh does not differ markedly from the culture found in the Indian state of West Bengal. The people of the Bengal region are of the Dravido-Aryan racial stock and share a similarity of language, dress, music and literature across the national boundaries. Certainly the Bengali passion for politics and poetry seems to spill across the border between the state of West Bengal in India and Bangladesh.

The *Jatra*, or folk theatre, is common at the village level, with dramas mainly portraying social or political themes. *Kabigan* is a form of folk debate conducted in verse. This is most common during festivals. Traditional Bangala music is gradually being subsumed by the cultural dominance of Indian music from across the border. The works of the great Bengali poets Rabindranath Tagore and Nazrul Islam, whose photos are somewhat curiously displayed in restaurants and barber shops, are kept alive only by intellectuals.

Election campaigns are probably the time when the general population assumes its most visible cultural excesses; villages, towns and whole districts become swathed in tri-colours and paper bunting, with posters proclaiming the promises and faces of the respective candidates. Truckloads of youthful supporters, driven around the countryside to attend speeches and rallies, march through the town shouting the name and qualities of the candidate people should vote for. It all becomes a bit torrid after a while, but it seems one of the few things the people readily join in.

FLORA & FAUNA
Like most of the northern flatlands of the subcontinent, Bangladesh is both subtropical and tropical. This has given rise to a great variety of flora and fauna.

Fauna
Wildlife offers most notably the jungle cats like the Royal Bengal Tiger and others of the cat family: cheetahs, leopards and panthers. Other large animals include the Asiatic elephant, the black bear, wild pigs and deer. Monkeys, otters and mongoose are among a few of the lesser-sized animals.

Reptiles include the sea tortoise, mud turtle, river tortoise, pythons, crocodiles and a variety of unpleasant poisonous snakes. Marine life includes a wide variety of both river and sea fish.

Birdlife offers over 500 varieties, two-thirds of which are resident species. Perhaps the best known bird species, though not often associated with Bangladesh, is the mynah of which there are six different varieties. The migratory and seasonal birds are predominantly ducks, which are hunted on the flooded fields.

Flora
Apart from a few regions where the great plantations of cash crops have replaced the indigenous varieties, there is still a good amount of original vegetation. Any land, however, that can be turned over to cultivation is drained and planted with some crop or other. Consequently, the best regions to sample the native plantlife are in the swamp regions of the Meghna Depression.

The forests of Bangladesh still cover 15% of the country, half of this in the Chittagong Hill Tracts district and a further quarter in the Sundarbans, the rest scattered in small pockets through the country. The forests fall distinctly into three regional varieties: the mangrove forests of the tidal zones along the coast; the inland or sal forests, so named for the sal tree which predominates in the Dacca, Tangail and Mymensingh districts; the upland forests, found in the Chittagong Hill Tracts and parts of Sylhet. These consist of tropical and semi-tropical evergreens.

ARCHITECTURE
4th-2nd century BC: Pre-Mauryan & Mauryan The term *bangala* comes from the indigenous architecture of this period. The bamboo thatched hut with a distinctively curved roof, still seen in villages today, known as a *bangala*, is the most ancient architectural form known in the country.

Chinese annals mention that as early as the 5th century AD Bangala, as it was known, was a prosperous Buddhist country, replete with many stupas, temples and monasteries, all made of bricks.

4th-8th century AD: Gupta Buddhist The traditional design of a stupa for this period consisted of a square plinth surmounted by a circular one and topped by a solid dome which tapers off sharply near the top. The traditional design of the cell which the monks lived in, a little three-metre-square cube was established during this period. The only variation was the addition of an ornamental pedestal placed in a few cells, like those found in Paharpur.

The great brick temples and monasteries were already in existence during this time. The temples at Mahastanagar, Comilla and Noakhali were mentioned by the Chinese traveller Xuan Zhang in the 7th century. It is not known if the great Paharpur temple was in existence at that time. Apart from a similar temple in Bihar in India there is no other temple of a similar cruciform design. This design appears to be purely indigenous to the Bengal region but the terracotta artwork with friezes of people at their daily chores and wildlife in its natural habitat is certainly an indigenous design.

Architecture seems to have fallen from favour during the Pala period because no important structures either Buddhist or Hindu have been discovered from this era.

12th-13th centuries: Sena Dynasty During this period Hindu temples were constructed with a pronounced Indian influence. Perfect specimens are to be found in Petua in the district of Rajshahi. Much later the Indian design of Hindu temples was replaced by purely indigenous architecture. The temple in Kantanagar in the Dinajpur district is a good example.

Muslim Period From the 12th through to the 16th century a variety of Muslim styles, generally marked by a rough approach to construction, penetrated the architecture of the region.

The Turkestan Khiljis period from 1202 to the 15th century is noted mainly for its mosques such as the Mazhar of Ghiazzuddin Azam Shah (1399-1440) in Mograpara in Sonargaon; the Sat Gombad Mosque and Mazhar of Khan Jahan Ali (1459) in Bagerhat in the Khulna district; the Baba Adam Mosque in Dacca; the Sura Mosque (1493-1538) in the district of Dinajpur; the Qubt Mosque in the district of Mymensingh; and the Khewa Mosque (1582) in Sherpur in the Bogra district. The short Afghan period from 1520 to 1576 followed the same Turkish design as the mosques in Sonargaon.

From 1576 to 1757 the Moghuls ruled Bangala and made some improvements on the simple design of preceding Muslim architecture although they did not follow the traditional designs employed in India. Notable specimens are the Bora Katra and Chotto Katra in Dacca (17th century); the Tomb of Pari Bibi in the Lalbagh Fort, Dacca (17th century); the river forts at Idrakpur in the Munshinganj district; and the Hadjiganj and Sonakonda in Narayanganj district. The only marble work by the Moghuls is the Tomb of Pari Bibi.

The Portuguese The Portuguese introduced European renaissance architecture via their colony in Goa. Palaces during this period took on a baroque style.

British Raj The renaissance style introduced by the Portuguese was continued by the British in such buildings as the Ahsan Manzil on the Bund in Dacca, the old State Bank building in Saddarghat, and the old High Court building in the same area.

In the 18th and 19th century the traditional British architecture was introduced. Good examples are the residential buildings on Top Khana Rd in Dacca. Other perfect specimens of purely British architecture are found in Rajshahi, like the Rajshahi College. Later the Victorian-Moghul style was followed, most loudly demonstrated by North Brooke Hall and Curzon Hall, both in Dacca. Other examples are the Medical College and Science buildings, the Old Secretariat, the Defense Buildings and the Supreme Court, originally constructed as the governor's residence.

Modern Buildings Notable modern buildings in Bangladesh include the Gana Bhavan in Dacca with its geometric lines and shapes and the Baitul Moharram Mosque with its orthodox Islamic architecture interpreted with very sharp and spare lines.

LANGUAGE
The language of Bangladesh is officially

referred to as Bangala or Bangla but the term Bengali is frequently used. Like most of the languages of the subcontinent, Bengali is sanskrit-based and is to a remarkable degree similar to Hindi, but with a slight variation in pronunciation. 'A' as in *bara* (big) in Hindi is 'O' as in *bora* in Bangladesh. Similarly *chotto* (small) is pronounced *chotta* in Bengali. *Paisa* in Hindi is pronounced *poisa*; *dahi* (yoghurt) is *dhoi*. Hard vowels in Hindi, like *nobe* (ninety) become softer like *noboi*. Some consonants are aspirated, as in *panj* (five) which becomes *pa'ch*, like in French.

The sentence structure is similar to Latin, French, Japanese and German – subject-object-verb. Thus *apni Dacca jabo* – you to Dacca go.

English used to be fairly common, but not anymore. Nationalism stirred up a strong ethnocentrism, leaving English and many of the vestiges of the Raj as its victim. Hindi and Urdu likewise have fallen into disuse. There are virtually no signboards in English anywhere except in the modern commercial areas of Dacca and Chittagong. Still just a little effort will usually be repaid – simply asking *Chitt-agong bas?* will result in somebody pointing out which bus goes to Chittagong.

Bengali has a number of regional variations, but it is essentially the same throughout the country.

Useful Words & Phrases
Greetings

The flowery Islamic greetings are the correct form although the everyday *namaste* of the subcontinent is also commonly used. *Namaste* is the everyday greeting of both Hindi and Nepali.

Peace be unto you	*Asallah malaikhum*
Unto you, also peace (reply)	*Malaikhum salam*
Good morning	*Suprabhat*
Good evening	*Suprasundha*
Good night	*Suprarath*
How are you?	*Kaemon achen?*
I am well	*Balo achi*

Thank you	*Donnobad*
Goodbye	*Khudahafiz*
See you later	*Pore dekha hobe*
See you again	*Abadeka hobe*

The Basics

yes	*gee*
no	*nay*
good	*baro*
bad	*karap*
very	*kho*
enough	*jat estho* or *bas*
thing	*jesish*
open	*bikri*
closed	*bondo*
far	*dur*
near	*ghar*
new	*nuttan*
old	*puranna*
quick	*taratari*
slow	*ashte-ashte*
high	*ocho*
low	*nicho*
cold	*tanda*
hot	*goram*
more	*aro*
nice	*shundur*
eat	*khabo*
here	*ekane*
there	*okane*
know	*janen*
go	*jabo*
write	*likha*
see	*dekho*
look	*dekhao*
where	*khotai*
when	*khogoun*
what/how	*khoto*
weather	*abakhoya*
friend	*bondhu*
worker	*sramik*
farmer	*kirshak*
pond	*pukkur* (small)
	dighi (large)
dyke	*dikhi*
day	*din*
morning	*chokal*
afternoon	*bikhel*
evening	*rathu*
today	*adj*

tomorrow	*kalke*
yesterday	*gote kal*

Pronouns

I/We	*Ami*
You	*Apni*
He/She	*Chay*
They	*Tobachara*

Transport

boat	*noukha*
bus	*bas*
train	*tren*
autorickshaw	*babytaxi*

Food

food	*kabhar*
rice	*bhat*
bread	*roti*
tea	*cha*
water	*pani*
breakfast	*nashta*
sugar	*chini*
salt	*lobon*
chilli	*moris*
egg	*deem*
milk	*duod*
yoghurt	*dhoi*
mutton	*khazir*
meat	*mangsa/gosht*
chicken	*murgi*
beef	*gorur*

Common Phrases

How much?
  Dom khoto?
How much is this?
  Eta — dom khoto?
Where are you going?
  Khotai jaben?
I am going to the YMCA
  YMCA jaichi
What time is the bus leaving?
  Eta bas khotai jabe?
What is the time?
  Khoto bajha?
I go
  jai
I want to go to Dacca
  Ami Dacca jabo

Do you speak Bangala?
  Apni Bangala janen?
I am going to Chittagong this afternoon
  Adj bikhele Chittagong jabo
I want to eat
  Ami kabhar lagbi
What do you want?
  Khabo?
Where is the post office?
  Post office khotai?
You smoke?
  Cigarette khaben?
It is available
  Pawa jai
Not available
  Pawa jaina

Numbers

Counting up to 20 is easy, but after this it becomes complicated as the terms are not sequential. In Bengali 21 is not *bis-ek* or *ek-bis* but *ekhus*; 45 is not *chollish-pa'ch* or *pa'ch-chollish* but *poy-chollish*. It's much easier to write these larger numbers down.

1	১	*ek*
2	২	*dui*
3	৩	*teen*
4	৪	*char*
5	৫	*pa'ch*
6	৬	*choy*
7	৭	*sa'ath*
8	৮	*ath*
9	৯	*noe*
10	১০	*dos*
11	১১	*ekaro*
12	১২	*baro*
13	১৩	*tero*
14	১৪	*chodo*
15	১৫	*pa'chro*
16	১৬	*chorto*
17	১৭	*shutaro*
18	১৮	*atharo*
19	১৯	*unish*
20	২০	*bis/kuri*
30	৩০	*tiris*
40	৪০	*chollish*
50	৫০	*po'chas*
60	৬০	*choyet*

70	৭০	*chattar*
80	৮০	*ashi*
90	৯০	*noboi*
100		*ek sou*
1000		*ek azhar*
100,000		*ek lakh*
10,000,000		*ek crore*
½		*chare*
¼		*choa*
¾		*pone*
1½		*derta*
2½		*arai*

GOVERNMENT

Based on a French model, Bangladesh is constitutionally defined as a secular socialist democracy, headed by a president. Although 80% of the population is Muslim, the secular nature of the government is written into the constitution. Unlike many other Islamic countries, the Muslim clergy, the mullahs, do not hold sway over national politics.

Since March 1982, democratic government in Bangladesh has been suspended following the coup by Lieutenant-General Ershad. He has ruled with a mixed cabinet of diplomats, politicians and army officers. General Ershad pledged a return to democracy in 1984, but he held a referendum on whether or not he should hold an election instead.

Administratively, the country is divided into four divisions: Dacca, Chittagong, Rajshahi and Khulna. Each division is in turn divided into 20 districts, 62 sub-divisions, 66,000 *thanas* (an administrative unit which loosely translates as 'police station'). Other units are *upazilas* (local councils) and *parishads*.

The socialist bent of the government has been modified over recent years, motivated out of the sheer need to survive. The nationalisation of industry and commerce has been wholly revoked, with inducements to lure back former foreign owners.

Internationally, Bangladesh is a non-aligned state, a member of the Commonwealth, the UNO and the Economic and Social Commission for Asia and the Pacific.

Facts for the Visitor

VISAS

For Commonwealth countries, no visa is required except for citizens of India, Canada, UK, Australia and Sri Lanka. Note that some Australian and Canadian passport holders have been told by Bangladesh consular offices in Bangkok and Calcutta they don't need visas: they do, despite what they are told. No visa is required for a 90-day stay for nationals of Japan, South Korea and Yugoslavia.

A 72-hour transit visa is usually granted for those arriving without any visa. A seven-day tourist visa is also available. If you wish to stay longer the 72-hour or the seven-day visa can usually be extended. You must first register at the Special Branch Office located in the Malibagh Bazar area on Kakrail Rd in Dacca then go to the Immigration Office.

Extensions Apply at the Immigration & Passport Office, 30 New Circuit House Rd, Dacca, with two passport photos. The office is open from 8 to 11 am and extensions are usually delivered by 1 to 2 pm on the same day for routine applications. The offices is closed on Fridays. Usually the stay is extended by two weeks but longer extensions are possible although they may take longer. A month extension may entail a week-long wait. Longer than a month can take at least two weeks to a month.

Fees for visa extensions vary according to nationality. Remember (see above) that if you only have a 72-hour transit visa or a seven-day visa, because you arrived in the country without any visa, you first have to apply to the Special Branch Office before going to the Immigration Office.

Bangladesh Embassies

Australia
  43 Hampton Circuit, Yarralumla, ACT 2600 (tel 811 4444, 811 8000).

Belgium
  27 rue Baron de Castro, 1040 Brussels (tel 7349950, 7349930).

Brazil
  Hig-sul. Avenida W-3, Quadra 705, Block A, Casa 19, 70.000 Brasilia-DF (tel 428925).

Burma
  340 Prome Rd, Rangoon (tel 17855, 17147). Consulate: Strand Rd, Akyab (tel 126).

Canada
  85 Range Rd, Suite No 402, Ottawa KIN 8J6 (tel 236 0138, 236 0139).

France
  5 Avenue Victor Hugo (5th floor), Paris 75116 (tel 704 03434, 727 6352).

Germany (East)
  Clara-zetkin Strasse 97/v, 108 Berlin (tel 229 2522, 229 1795).

Germany (West)
  Bonnerstrasse 48, 5300 Bonn-Bad Godesberg (tel 35 3071-2)

Hong Kong
  Consulate: Room 1401, Harbour Hotel, 116 Gloucester Rd (tel 743-211-16)

India
  56 Ring Rd, Lajpat Nagar 111, New Delhi (tel 61-5668, 61-9257). Consulate: 9 Circus Avenue, Calcutta 17 (tel 44-5208, 44-5209). Consulate: 9 Kunjaban Rd, Agartala (tel 1287).

Italy
  Via Antonio Bertoloni 14, 00197 Rome (tel 80 3595, 87 8541)

Great Britain
  28 Queens Gate, London SW7 5JA (tel 01 584 0081, 01 589 4842)

Nepal
  21/490 Kalikasthan Dilli Bazar, Kathmandu (tel 13509)

Pakistan
  House 21, Street No 88, Ataturk Avenue, Ramna 6/3, Islamabad (tel 25218-9) Trade Commission: Hotel Metropole, Room 27, Karachi (tel 51 5496)

Sweden
  26-Grov Turegatan 11438, Stockholm (tel 605501, 605511, 625591).

Switzerland
  7 rue Henry Veyrassat, 1202 Geneva (tel 449340, 449349).

Thailand
  Phatra Tanakit (Firestone Building), 4th
  floor, 183 Sukhumvit Rd, Bangkok (tel
  2511132)
United Nations
  130 East 40th St, 5th floor, New York, NY
  10016 (tel 212 686 5233-4).
USA
  3421 Massachussetts Avenue NW, Washing-
  ton DC 20007 (tel 202 337 6644 5 6).
USSR
  6-Zemledelcheski Perelek, Moscow (tel
  246 79 00).

CUSTOMS

A Customs Declaration Form is issued on
arrival. Keep this until you leave as
officials will check this before they let you
out of the country.

Tourists are allowed to bring in 200
cigarettes or two cartons and two litres or
two bottles of liquor. The old selling-the-
duty-frees game isn't crash hot in Bangladesh and if you do get involved take care
as some of the dealers are less than
straightforward. Recently some travellers
have also been talked into buying betel
nut in Burma to resell in Bangladesh.
That's unlikely to work either! Around the
Biman office and the Dacca Sheraton
Hotel are prime areas for selling goods.

MONEY

The principal unit of money is the takka
(Tk) which is divided up into one hundred
poisas.

A$1	= Tk 19
US$1	= Tk 27
£1	= Tk 37
1 DM	= Tk 10

The blackmarket in Bangladesh is not
very active nor very profitable for those
who wish to use it. Even the resale value of
duty-free goods such as whiskey and
cigarettes is not very high.

A currency declaration form is given to
you on arrival and you must use this when
changing foreign currency or travellers'
cheques. Keep this until departure as
customs officials check it before you are
allowed to leave.

On departure tourists are allowed to
reconvert Tk 500 into foreign currency or
25% of the total foreign currency encashed
in the country. If you require cash US
dollars, banks are allowed to give you
US$50 when cashing a foreign travellers'
cheque.

If you need to have money transferred
to you in Bangladesh allow plenty of time
and choose a good bank. To convert a
bankdraft into travellers' cheques find a
bank that has some relationship with
yours, or do it through someone who does.
This avoids the bank's commission or
service fee.

Despite the poverty in Bangladesh
crime is surprisingly low. Even pick-
pocketing on the crowded buses is not as
endemic as in some other Asian countries.
Nor is baksheesh, that almost universal
custom of equitable redistribution of
wealth by means of asking for it, particularly aggressive in Bangladesh compared to
India. There are, however, plenty of beggars.

Coping with Beggars

Beggars are everywhere in Bangladesh
and in such abject condition that it is
reminiscent of India 20 years ago. There
are those so terribly deformed or miss-
hapen that they are almost lifeless and, at
the other extreme, there are urchins,
particularly in Chittagong, who fling back
coins and cluster around tourists demanding paper money! It is certainly arguable
that you leave them no better and no
worse but equally it helps the conscience a
little to dole some out to the really needy.

CLIMATE

The climate of Bangladesh is sub-tropical
and tropical with temperatures ranging
from a daytime low of 21°C in the cold
season to a top of 35°C in the hot season.
Annual rainfall varies from 1000 mm (50
inches) in the west to 2500 mm in the
south-east and up to 5000 mm in the
submontane region of the hills of Assam.

Three-quarters of the annual rainfall occurs between June and September. The 90-95% humidity in the hot season makes many parts of the country almost unbearable until the monsoon season comes along.

Bangladesh, on average, is affected 16 times a decade by cyclones which form in the Bay of Bengal during the monsoon season. These tropical cyclones hit the coast, usually between Calcutta and Cox's Bazar, with winds of up to 100 kmph and storm tides that wreak havoc on coastal plains and villages. The worst cyclone in recent times was in November 1970 when 225,000 people were killed and more than US$50 million worth of damage was caused. The cyclone of June 1985 also caused severe loss of life and great damage.

Bangladesh has three main seasons: the monsoon or 'wet' season from mid-June to mid-October; the 'cold' season from mid-October to the end of February; and the 'hot' season – known in Bangladesh as the 'little rainy season' – from March to the end of May.

The best time to visit Bangladesh is in the cold season when the weather is dry and fresh. The days are sunny, with clear blue skies and the countryside is green after the monsoon rains. Temperatures range from 10°C overnight to 21°C during the day and rainfall is negligible.

The beginning of the hot season is reasonably pleasant with tolerable humidity, warm days and nights and clear skies. But by mid-April, as the monsoon approaches, the temperature rises to 35°C during the day and 29°C overnight. With 90-95% humidity, this time of the year can be almost intolerable. Dangerously heavy hailstorms are also quite common, with reports of some hail stones weighing half a kilogram. The winds that provide this unusual weather whirl up from the Bay of Bengal then U-turn at the Himalaya and carry their icy cargo back to Bangladesh. They are known as *guarni jour*. By the end of May, after a period of heavy 'advance-warning' downpours, the monsoon finally breaks.

The average starting date for the monsoon in Bangladesh is 15 June though it can be up to three weeks earlier or later. It doesn't rain solidly all day every day but tends to be an initial downpour, followed by clear skies. The air feels lighter, cleaner and sweeter-smelling and the rain appears to relieve the oppressive heat.

Although there are only three observable seasons in Bangladesh, the locals have six; *Basato* (spring) – from March to April; *Barsha* (rainy) – May to June; *Grisha* (summer) – July to August; *Hemonto* (autumn) – September to October; *Sarat* (misty) – November to December; and *Seet* (winter) – January to February.

HEALTH

Inoculations For entry most travellers are required to have a valid International Health Certificate for cholera and typhoid. These can be given jointly as TABC, which protects against typhoid, paratyphoid A and B and cholera. Vaccinations against smallpox is no longer required by the Bangladesh government as the disease has been wiped out worldwide. It's a good idea to ensure that your tetanus inoculation is up to date, along with a booster for polio; a gamma globulin inoculation against infectious hepatitis is a good idea, as is the recently available human-diploid-cell rabies vaccine. For those travelling overland, a plague inoculation is recommended. Yellow fever protection is only obligatory for people visiting from central Africa or northern South America.

Malaria
Malarial risk in Bangladesh is supposed to be restricted to the Chittagong and Chittagong Hill Tracts areas; no one as yet has told the mosquitoes.

It is not (yet) possible to be vaccinated against malaria, but it is absolutely necessary to take precautions against it while you are in Bangladesh. Malaria is spread by mosquitoes and the disease has a nasty habit of coming back in later years even if you are cured at the time – and it can be fatal. Protection is simple – a daily or weekly tablet depending on which your doctor recommends.

Pregnant women should not take chloroquine (daily) tablets. Some doctors recommend Proguanil as the best anti-malarial for pregnancy. When travelling with very small children try to avoid using daily tablets – getting a tablet into a small child every day of the week is not a pleasant task. Anti-malarials in a syrup form are now available for children.

Stomach Problems

The usual health problem afflicting visitors to any part of the subcontinent is some form of upset stomach. Often this can be due simply to a change of diet or a system unused to spicy food. Many times, however, contaminated food or water is the problem.

There are two answers to the upset stomach problem. First avoid getting it in the first place by taking care of what you eat and drink. Uncooked foods are always more likely to harbour germs but so are cooked foods once they have been allowed to cool. Try to eat only freshly cooked foods and beware of places where food is left sitting around for long periods, particularly if exposed to flies. The fresher and the hotter the better is a good rule.

The main cause of upset stomachs is probably drinking untreated water – the answer is to either drink hot tea or bottled soft drinks from reputable bottlers. This doesn't always work in the thirsty hot season so if you must drink water try to either have it boiled or carry water purification tablets. These are available from pharmacies in the west or, with more difficulty, locally. Water is more effectively sterilised by iodine solution than by tablets – it kills amoebic cysts as well but does require practice drinking swimming pool water. Even in good hotels 'drinking water' may be just filtered, not boiled.

Take care with local food too – eat only at places that look reasonably clean and where the food is well prepared. Particularly avoid sidewalk ice cream vendors and fresh salads. Fruit is generally OK as long as it can be peeled.

If avoidance fails and you do get a stomach bug the first thing to do is nothing. If you can simply get back to health by yourself you'll probably build up some immunity against it recurring. People who take antibiotics at the first sign of an upset stomach are only asking for trouble. Not only does it make another assault more difficult to repel, it also kills off the useful organisms in your digestive tract just as efficiently as it kills off the harmful ones.

Local Problems

Travellers should beware of the usual tropical health problems. The heat, but more important the excessive humidity, is likely to sap your energy and predispose you to other health problems. Keep cool is the answer! In this climate small cuts and scratches can very easily become infected – treat any injury, no matter how minor, with exaggerated caution. The quality of local food is also likely to be less than western visitors are used to and you should be wary not to get run down due to poor nutrition.

Medical Facilities

Doctors are good, but nursing and ancillary care is not up to western standards. There were over 8000 doctors in 1982, but only 2000 registered nurses to serve some 130 hospitals. Relative to the population these figures are terrible – only one doctor for every 40,000 people. Nevertheless health standards have measurably improved in Bangladesh in recent years.

The best hospitals are the Post-graduate and the Holy Family in Dacca. Civilians and tourists can also be treated in the military hospitals.

ACCOMMODATION

Although there are now international standard hotels in Dacca most accommodation in Bangladesh is well down the price scale. Although you can find very cheap places you get what you pay for; the really rock bottom hotels are likely to have bed bugs as standard equipment. One couple reported that they reckoned you had to pay Tk 60-80 to get reasonable standard places.

The Bangladesh Parjatan Corporation, the national tourist corporation, also manages a number of modern motels throughout the country. A few middle level class hotels have begun to appear with modern, clean facilities, but these tend to be correspondingly pricey. The common boarding house, a legacy from the British Raj when they were guest houses, remains but only in a fairly run down fashion. Some, however, are being renovated, so things may improve.

FOOD

The food of Bangladesh is, like the rest of the subcontinent, influenced by the regional variations of its history. Bangladesh, once an outpost of the Moghul empire, now retains this part of its heritage through its cuisine. Kebabs and koftes of all kinds are available. This has combined to form a curious mix with the more southern, vegetarian cuisine plus the many Chinese restaurants found in the cities.

The three main forms of rice dishes which you're likely to encounter are the biryani, rice with chicken or beef or mutton; pulao, spiced like the biryani but without the meat; baht which is just plain rice. Chicken tikka and chicken kebabs are also common. They are usually served with Persian-style nan (bread) or with Persian rice which is usually prepared with butter. Purely local food is mainly rice, vegetables, dhal and Indian-style chappatis and chillis.

Seafood is common. The fish – broiled, smoked or fried – you are most likely to eat is probably the hilsa. Prawns and crabs are also available, but along with lobsters are only to be found in the better restaurants in Dacca and Chittagong. Kebabs come in a wide variety include sheesh kebab, with is prepared with less spice and usually with mutton or beef, and shami kebab, made with fried minced meat. Koftes are minced meatballs cooked in gravy.

Desserts

The Bangladeshis have a sweet-tooth and many sugar-loaded desserts are made. Even their yoghurt, known as mesti dhoi, is sweetened. It's virtually impossible to get normal fresh yoghurt. Other sweet things include:

halva – a common dessert ranging from egg halva to carrot, sooji or wheat cream, almond, pistachio nuts, and so on.
sundesh – a milk-based dessert, one of the best available.
zorda – sweetened rice with nuts.
firni – rice flour cooked in milk, sugar and flavouring.
pitha – a blanket term for cakes or pastries including specific varieties such as chitoi, dhupi, takti, andosha, puli, barfi and pua.
rasgula & kalojam – two popular Indian-style desserts, milk-based and made with sugar, flour and ghee.
keora – a milk and sugar combination flavoured with a floral extract, usually rose.
rose malai – round sweets floating in a thick milk.
molidhana – another milk-based dessert similar to halva.

Fruits include bananas, mangoes, papayas, jackfruit, watermelon, pineapple and lychees. There are no oranges, only tangerines.

Snacks

Local 'fastfoods' are plentiful, some of the more common include:

samosa – a batter-covered triangle of vegetable and meat. In Bangala they are known as *sringala*.

aloe – a potato-vegetable 'chop', pear-shaped and fried.

puri – a tortilla-like preparation of potato, minced meat and vegetables, can be rather greasy.

moghlai paratha – a type of Indian bread prepared with flour and eggs and usually served for breakfast.

luchis – a tasty and crusty fried vegetable preparation.

Chinese Restaurants

Dacca has a vast array of Chinese restaurants, so numerous that they are the dominant culinary form in this city. Almost all are run by locals who have received some level of Chinese tuition. Those that are run by ethnic Chinese are distinguished by the smaller servings but higher quality. There are a few other restaurants claiming to serve Japanese, Italian or French food – usually just a local approximation.

Drinks

The milky sweet tea known as *chai* is everywhere, but don't expect to be able to get coffee anywhere apart from a few modern restaurants. *Lassi*, the refreshing yoghurt drink, is also uncommon. Coconut milk is a fine, safe and refreshing drink. A whole young coconut costs about Tk 3. International soft drinks, such as Pepsi, Coke and Fanta, are readily available and cost about Tk 5-6. Getting them cold is not so easy, they're much more likely to be served 'boiled', ie warm!

There is no problem finding alcoholic drinks in Bangladesh, except that anything foreign is expensive. Local drinks are available in licensed wine-shops at a much lower rate. In Dacca beer prices go up with the name of the hotel – in Dacca clubs a beer costs Tk 30, in the Hotel Purbani Tk 50, in the Dacca Sheraton Tk 60 and in the Hotel Sonargaon Tk 80.

In the countryside you may encounter a drink called *tari*, made from coconuts. When it is fresh, it is cool and sweet; but when it is fermented it becomes the local beer. It is universally known as 'coconut toddy', but only found in non-Muslim areas like the Chittagong Hill Tracts. *Kesare rose* is the rural liqueur, made from date molasses. It is mixed with hot water and tastes like brandy or cognac. A soft drink bottleful costs Tk 8.

TOURIST INFORMATION

The Bangladesh Parjatan Corporation is the national Bangladesh tourist office. They provide tourist information and also run accommodation and tours in several locales. They have a number of interesting brochures about Bangladesh. Their offices in the country are:

Dacca
    Main Office: Old Airport Building, Tezgaon, Dacca 15 (tel 325155-59)
    Zia International Airport (tel 609416)
    Hotel Dacca Sheraton (tel 509479)
    Hotel Sonargaon (tel 315071-95)
Chittagong
    Motel Shaikat Building, Station Rd (tel 209514, 204650)
Cox's Bazar
    Motel Upal (tel 246)
Rajshahi
    Parjatan Motel (tel 2392)
Rangamati
    Parjatan Motel, Deer Park (tel 236, 366)
Kaptai
    Motel Panthapriya (tel 40)
Khulna
    Hotel Selim Building, Shamsur Rahman Rd (tel 24711)
Bogra
    Masud Hall Sutrapur (tel 5651)
    Court Rd (tel 2392)

FOREIGN EMBASSIES

Since Bangladesh is hardly on the beaten track embassies are not as unhappy to see their nationals as they appear to be in busier locations. Travellers (at least British and Australian ones) have reported even being able to read the newspapers, get a cold beer *and* use the swimming pool at their embassy.

Top: snakeskin vendors, Sylhet, Chittagong Division (JRS)
Left: little girl, Sat Gombad, Bagerhat, Khulna Division (JRS)
Right: preparing chillis on a ferry, rivertrip to Dacca (JRS)

Top: boat heavily laden with rice straw (GW)
Bottom: boats and boys at Chilmari (GW)

The main embassies travellers are likely to have to deal with are those from neighbouring countries for which visas may be required – that is Burma, India, Nepal and Thailand. Details are as follows:

Burma – The embassy (tel 601915-1) is at Rd No 4, House No 89B, Banani Area, diplomatic enclave. See the Thailand embassy details below for how to get there. The embassy is open 9.30 am to 1 pm and visas are obtainable within 24 hours. Two passport photos, production of a ticket out of Burma and the appropriate fee are required.

India – The high commission (tel 313606) is at Rd No 2, House No 120, Dhanmondi Residential Area. The office is open 9.30 to 11.30 am only and visas can be collected the next day between 4 and 5 pm. The office is closed on Fridays and Saturdays. Two passport photos and the appropriate fee are required. Travel permits to Siliguri and Darjeeling can also be obtained here within 24 hours. Again two passport photos are required but there is no fee.

Nepal – The embassy (tel 312907) is at Lake Rd No 2, Baridhara Rd, Gulshan-2. The office is open 9.30 am to 4 pm and visas are issued within 24 hours. Two passport photos and a Tk 250 fee are required. It is possible to enter Nepal without a visa and be issued with a seven-day visa on arrival but the fee is similar and extending the visa in Kathmandu beyond seven days is simple but time consuming.

Thailand – The embassy (tel 601915-1) is at Rd No 18, House No 21 in the same Banani area as the Burmese embassy. Take a bus No 6 at Farm Gate and get off at the last bus stop, it is then a five-minute walk to either embassy. The embassy is open 9.30 am to 1 pm, visas are issued in 24 hours and two passport photos and a fee are required.

Other diplomatic offices in Dacca include:

Australia
    184 Gulshan Avenue, Gulshan, tel 600091-5
Belgium
    House No 40, Rd No 21, Block B, Banani, tel 600138
Canada
    House No 16A, Rd No 48, Gulshan, tel 600181-5
France
    House No 18, Rd No 108, Gulshan, tel 600286
Iran
    171 Gulshan Avenue, Gulshan, tel 601096
Italy
    House No NWD4, Rd 58/62, Gulshan, tel 602159
Japan
    House No 110, Rd No 27, Block A, Banani, tel 312949
Netherlands
    House No 49, Rd No 90, Gulshan, tel 600279
Sweden
    73 Gulshan Avenue, Gulshan, tel 600461
UK
    DIT Building Annexe, 5th floor, Dilkusha Commercial Area, tel 243251-3, 244216-7
USA
    Adamjee Court 115/20, Motijheel Commercial Area, tel 244220
West Germany
    178 Gulshan Avenue, Gulshan, tel 600166

GENERAL INFORMATION
Post & Telecommunications
The GPO Post Restante service is efficient.

Telegraph and telephone services are linked with all major regions of the world. International trunk calls are often more efficient than domestic calls. You can actually hear!

Electricity
220 volts in major urban areas; a variety can be found in the provinces.

Office Hours
Banking hours are 9 am to 1 pm, Sunday to Thursday. The weekend is Friday and

Saturday. Government office hours are 9 am to 5 pm, Sunday to Wednesday, 9 am to 2 pm on Thursday. Shopping hours are 10 am to 8 pm.

MEDIA

There are two English language newspapers, the *Bangladesh Times* and the *Bangladesh Observer* and one English language weekly, *The Holiday*.

There is a TV station in Dacca with broadcasts from Chittagong, Natore, Khulna, Sylhet, Rangpur, Rangamati, Cox's Bazar and Mymensingh.

BOOKS & MAPS

There's remarkably little published in the west about Bangladesh. Other guidebooks to the country are limited to *Bangladesh – A Traveller's Guide* by Don Yeo (Roger Lascelles, London) and the short section on Bangladesh in *A Handbook for Travellers in India, Nepal, Pakistan, Bangladesh & Sri Lanka* (John Murray, London).

Bangladesh by B L Johnson (Heinemann Educational Books, London) is one of the few general books on the country published in the west. Most histories of Bangladesh or the Bengal region are published either in Dacca or Calcutta. Titles include:

Historical Geography of Ancient & Early Medieval Bengal, Amitabha Bhattarcharya, Calcutta
Tribal Culture in Bangladesh, Abdus Sattar, Dacca
An Economic Geography of Bangladesh, Haroun El Rashid
The History of Bengal 1200-1757, J N Sakkar
British Policy & the Muslim in Bengal, Azizur Rahman Mallick
Glimpses of Old Dacca, S M Tarfu, Calcutta

General books which might be worth consulting before visiting Bangladesh, include travel health guides like the *Traveller's Health Guide* by Dr A C Turner (Roger Lascelles, London) or *Staying Healthy in Asia* (Volunteers in Asia Publications). *The Tropical Traveller* by John Hatt (Pan London) is a good general introduction to tropical travel.

Maps for Bangladesh are equally limited. Bartholomew's map of *India, Pakistan, Nepal, Bangladesh & Sri Lanka* is about the best available for Bangladesh but it's far too small scale to be really useful. The Parjatan *Bangladesh Tourist Map* is larger scale but far too inaccurate to be useful.

TRAVELLERS' IMPRESSIONS

Whether their visit was weeks, years or centuries ago travellers' interests seem to be the same – the prices, the climate, the people, the curiosities and so on. Some impressions of Bangladesh:

Fa Hsien – A 5th century Chinese Buddhist pilgrim, Fa Hsien came here via the Karakorams where the Gupta imperial power extended. He visited Buddhist pilgrimage centres in northern India and was impressed all the way through by the great structures and the prosperity of the land.

Xuan Zhang – Another Chinese Buddhist traveller he also came here via the Karakorams, but two centuries later. Xuan Zhang was similarly impressed by the numerous towering temples, stupas and large monasteries where thousands of bhikkus lived and which he described as, 'ornaments of the earth, as high as mountain peaks, obstructing the very course of the sun with their lofty and imposing towers.' He probably exaggerated a little.

Marco Polo – Travelling as an emissary of Kublai Khan in the 14th century the famed Venetian traveller came close to the southern borders of China but may never have actually visited Bangala. Hence his information certainly does not sound first-hand. He described Bangala as a province close to India and of southern China, populated by wretched idolaters with a peculiar language.

Ibn Battuta – A Moroccan from Tangier this 14th century visitor was particularly impressed with how inexpensive Bangala was. He stocked up on female slaves who seem to have been available at bargain basement prices that century. Of Bangala he wrote that: 'There are innumerable vessels on the rivers and each vessel carries a drum and when vessels meet each of them beats a drum and they salute one another.'

He visited Sylhet to see a famous Persian saint who lived in a cave and fasted for 10 days and drank cow's milk on the 11th. 'He would then remain standing all night in prayer.' The saint apparently said his prayers in Mecca each morning but was present in his cave the rest of the day. He also paid a special visit to Mecca each year on the occasion of the Id festival.

'We travelled down the river for 15 days (from Sylhet to Sonargaon),' wrote Ibn Battuta, 'between villages and orchards just as if we were going through a bazar. On the banks are waterwheels, orchards, villages to the right and left like those on the Nile River.' He discovered that there were numerous religious mendicants, sufis and fakirs and described the land as having an abundance of the essentials of life and as being scenic and luxuriant. In summer, he reported, the creeks and inlets steamed up and as they went through them they had a 'vapour bath'. The people in the west generally, he continued, were oppressed and called the land *Dazaki-i-pur Niamat* – a hell crammed with blessings.

Mu Huang – This Chinese traveller visited Sonargaon in the 15th century, probably as a seaman. He described foreign vessels arriving and lying at anchor in estuaries while small boats ferried them to the inland river port. He was similarly impressed by the general prosperity of the land, the cities with palaces, temples and gardens. Like Ibn Battuta he noted that there were many sufis and fakirs.

Zaheed Beg – In the 17th century this

Moghul visitor observed that no one liked the country. Moghul officials and military officers stationed here demanded increased salaries, higher ranks and payment in cash. It was an unhealthy land and Zaheed Beg, on being nominated as viceroy of Bangala, exclaimed: 'Ah . . . . your majesty could find no better place to kill me than Bangala.'

WHAT TO BRING

The weather is warm year round, you don't need to bring much clothing with you. Light, cotton clothing in summer; rainproof jacket for the monsoons; woollen pullover and jacket in winter. An umbrella can be useful at any time of the year, essential during the monsoon. Sandals or thongs are more comfortable than shoes although you'll probably want to be wearing shoes during the mad scramble to board buses!

THINGS TO BUY

Souvenirs in Bangladesh include jewellery, garments, brasswork, leatherwork, ceramics, jute products, artwork, woodcarvings and clay or metal sculptural work. Unique items include pink pearls, fine muslin, jamdani or silk saris, jute doormats, wall pieces, glass bangles, seashells and conch-shell bangles and reed mats. Craftsmanship is generally quite high and the prices are very low. An exception is jute carpets which are of low quality, quickly fade and are soon worn out.

CULTURAL PHENOMENA

Crowds are one thing any foreign traveller in Bangladesh will have to accustom themselves to. They appear wherever you may go, but are especially inquisitive in the rural areas where they are less likely to have seen white-skinned people before. If you don't want to find yourself in a situation beyond your control, don't play to them as they can easily get out of hand.

The 'thumbs-up' gesture carries a markedly different interpretation in Bangladesh than that understood in the west. Don't use it.

Despite these warnings, the people of Bangladesh are much friendlier than, in general, those across the border in India. Perhaps this is because English is spoken less.

Getting There

FLYING TO BANGLADESH

Although Dacca is far from being a major Asian crossroads there are plenty of flights there. Bangladesh Biman attract passengers by fare cutting – many travellers have used Dacca as the gateway to the subcontinent because of cheap fares from Europe. Biman are also a cheap way of travelling between South-East Asia and the subcontinent so many travellers fly through Dacca from Bangkok, Kathmandu or Rangoon to take advantage of Biman's competitive fares. Note, however, that fares out of Bangladesh are not such great bargains as fares *through* Bangladesh. A Biman ticket Bangkok-Dacca-London (bought in Singapore, Malaysia or Thailand) is likely to be a better deal than a simple Dacca-London ticket (bought in Bangladesh).

FROM EUROPE

Bangladesh Biman offer very competitive fares to Dacca from London. Typical prices would be around £200-250 one-way or £400 return. Alternatively you can fly to other Asian centres such as Calcutta or Bangkok and connect to Dacca from there. For cheap fares from London check the 'what's on' magazines like *Time Out*, the giveaway *Australasian Express* or the classified travel ads in papers like *The Times* or the *Telegraph*.

FROM THE USA

There are several ways to Bangladesh from the US. From the west coast you could fly to Bangkok and connect from there to Dacca. Alternatively you could fly direct to India and connect from there. From the US east coast another alternative would be to fly to London and get one of the cheap Biman flights from there direct to Dacca.

The network of student travel offices known as Council Travel are particularly good for cheap fares. Or check the Sunday travel sections of papers like the *New York Times* or the *Los Angeles Times* for travel agents advertising cheap fares. Typical fares from the west coast to Bangkok are around US$840 return, a bit more than half that one-way. Fares to Hong Kong are also a good bargain from around US$400 one-way, cheap fares are easy to obtain onwards from Hong Kong.

FROM AUSTRALIA

From Australia the simplest way to Bangladesh will be to fly to Bangkok in Thailand and fly from there to Dacca or to fly to Calcutta in India and fly or travel by land into Bangladesh. See the 'From Asia' section for more details of transport from Bangkok or Calcutta. Apex air fares from the Australian east coast to Bangkok are from A$632 one-way or A$971 return. With a little enquiring around the travel agents you should be able to find similar fares without the advance purchase restrictions. To Calcutta the advance purchase fares are A$1217 return, again you can hunt around travel agents for a better deal.

FROM ASIA

There are flights between all the neighbouring Asian countries – Thailand, Burma, India, Nepal, Pakistan – and Bangladesh. Apart from flights between Calcutta and Chittagong all connections are to Dacca International Airport.

India

There are daily Biman and Indian Airlines flights on the Calcutta-Dacca route; It is a one-hour flight with a fare of around US$36. Biman also fly Calcutta-Chittagong.

Nepal

Biman fly Kathmandu-Dacca twice weekly. There are also flights by Royal Nepal

Airways, and Pakistan International. Fare for the one-hour flight is around US$85.

Burma

There are flights once a week between Rangoon and Dacca with Biman. Typical fare for the 1½ hour flight is US$125.

Thailand

Thai International and Bangladesh Biman fly Bangkok-Dacca. Thai make the flight three times a week. The fare is typically around US$150.

Pakistan

Pakistan International Airlines fly between Karachi and Dacca.

FROM INDIA BY LAND

Although there are roads crossing between Bangladesh and India at a number of points along their long common border there are only two where you are actually permitted to cross – one for Calcutta and for Darjeeling. All the other border crossing points are officially closed. There are no open border crossing points between Bangladesh and Burma.

If, having entered by air, you leave via a land border crossing, a road permit is required. This can be obtained from the Immigration Office. Two passport photos are required but there is no fee. It's obtainable the same day if you apply for it in the morning.

Via Benopol: This is the main overland route into Bangladesh, made generally by train from Calcutta. It is a Rs 7 rickshaw ride to the immigration checkpost then walking distance to the actual border. Inside Bangladesh it is a Tk 4 rickshaw ride to the bus station in Benopol. See the Benopol section for more details.

Via Chiliharti: From Darjeeling to New Jalpaiguri takes 10 hours by the little train. A train from Siliguri to Haldibari is a two-hour trip and costs Rs 3.70 2nd class. There are three trains daily, the last at

5.30 pm. Note that you require a road permit from the Indian Embassy in Kathmandu or the Immigration Office in Delhi and Calcutta to travel through this area. It is advisable to take the early train as Haldibari is not a great place to stay, there are lots of mosquitoes.

There is a bus from Haldibari to Hemkumari, a border village, but it's slow and often late. An alternative is a rickshaw trip which takes two hours. From Hemkumari it is four km along a dirt road to Chiliharti, the first village on the Bangladesh side. This is all really academic, however, because this route is now officially closed and there is a watchtower to check on locals trying to sneak across into India. The road on the Indian side is now surfaced but the only legal and official route is an eight km walk along the old, and now unused, railway tracks via Haldibari to Hemkumari.

The immigration checkpost in Chiliharti is open from 10 am till 6 pm, but chances are that you might have to wait for the immigration officer who occasionally does not turn up on time. Keep a few rupees to change to takkas at the Indian border point for the train fare to Syedpur where you can then cash travellers' cheques.

In Syedpur it's worth having a good idea of your route through Bangladesh. The surrounding region has a number of interesting archaeological sites. To Dacca takes 12 to 14 hours – first by bus to Rangpur then by train via Mymensingh. Buses are in general faster overall. If you miss the last direct bus to Dacca, take a bus to Bogra (every hour, 2½ hour trip, Tk 13) where there is an hourly departure for Dacca. Bogra-Dacca takes six to eight hours, there are express and non-express buses and the fare is Tk 32.

Travelling north from Bangladesh into India the train from Syedpur to Chiliharti leaves at 3 pm and arrives at 6.15 pm. The fare is Tk 11 in 2nd class. In Chiliharti there's a guest house with rooms at Tk 30, but no electricity and it's wise to bring some of your own food. Across the border in India there is a *Dak Bungalow* in Haldibari which costs Rs 6.50. The train to Siliguri costs Rs 4 and departs at 7.30 am. Change trains at New Jalpaiguri where you also have to register at the Foreigner's Registration Office. Don't get off at the railway station in Siliguri, get off at the next station where the little Darjeeling trains depart at 7 and 9.30 am. The three-hour trip costs Rs 10.50.

A traveller's report on this crossing from India:

The Indian customs man at Haldibari (where we went after passport control – who looked as if they'd been sleeping for the past 10 years) told us with, it seemed to me, ill-concealed glee that he 'could not allow us to cross the border via the bus to Hemkumari as this route was closed.' It was 4.45 pm, mid-June and the monsoonal rain was threatening. The rickshaw man was demanding a higher price than the one we'd agreed upon (the old flinging the money to the ground, etc) and we felt so sick of India and the bureaucrats that we decided to walk the 10 km to Chiliharti.

The customs chap told us it was two km to the border – after half an hour or so we came to a removed bridge and had to walk through a thigh-deep warm rice-paddy-cum-stream. During this crossing the rain came and we were soaked to the skin within 10 seconds. But we made it to shelter! Then the rain stopped. The villagers were very friendly and mimed to us that there'd be one more shoes-off crossing in India.

It was very easy, pleasant walking, along the old railway through rice, jute and bamboo. I estimate it was four km from Indian customs at Haldibari to the Bangladesh border post. We never actually spotted the Indian border. In Bangladesh the bridges were still there so there was no wading through water. We walked from the border post (which was completely unmarked, the Bangladesh Defence Regiment came out to greet us) to Chilharti in an hour – a good fast pace set by the coolie we hired! As it was the next morning (no hotels or lodges, some kind Bengalis put us up) we were quite fresh. It

had taken us 1½ hours to walk from the Indian customs to the BDR compound (we assume it was the Bangladesh border), including a 20 minute delay due to rain, finding other shoes, reflecting, etc.

There's nowhere to change money in Chiliharti and the customs chap hassled us a bit because we, rather foolishly, claimed to have no takkas at all, thinking it was illegal to bring any into the country. You should have at least enough to get to Bogra. It took us two days of not terribly strenuous travel to get from the border to Dacca. Even the walk at the border is not so unpleasant – if you lash out a dollar on getting your ridiculously heavy pack carried.

Judith Tregear & David Murray-Smith

Via Tetulya: The map of this region is rather deceptive as it shows a road cutting across into Bangladesh from Siliguri in India via Tetulya. The road is certainly there but this route is closed and you are not permitted to enter or exit Bangladesh here. Immigration officials in Dacca are apparently not aware that the border crossing here is closed and are continuing to approve applications for road permits. There is no immigration or customs establishment on *either* side of the border, only an army cantonment. Apparently, however, the military personnel will sometimes let travellers through. It is hardly a route to recommend though.

Via Tamabil: This route from India is also closed, pending resolution of the unrest in Assam.

Via Akyab: This section of the Euro-Asian Highway, linking Bangladesh and Burma, has been closed since the early 1950s.

DEPARTING BANGLADESH

See the introductory section on money for details of currency reconversion restrictions. There is a Tk 200 airport tax on departure.

Getting Around

Internal transport in Bangladesh is very cheap, so cheap that everyone uses it all the time, whether it be air, land or water transport. The rule is if you want a seat get there early and learn to shove, kick and gouge like the rest of your travelling companions.

The distinguishing feature of internal travel in Bangladesh is the presence of a well developed and well used system of water transport. You will find that in a country where rivers and streams outstretch roads in total distance, water transport is not only very interesting but also unavoidable.

AIR

Biman, the national carrier, links all major towns and cities with Dacca. Domestic flights are government subsidised and tend to be cheaper than 1st-class train fares. There is a Tk 10 departure tax on internal flights.

from/to	freq	fare
Dacca/Chittagong	twice daily	Tk450
Dacca/Syedpur	four times a week	Tk 385
Dacca/Sylhet	three times a week	Tk 340
Dacca/Jessore	daily	Tk 310
Dacca/Ishurdi	four times a week	Tk 275
Dacca/Rajshahi	twice a week	Tk 275
Dacca/Cox's Bazar	twice a week	Tk 500
Chittagong/Cox's Bazar	twice a week	Tk 145

There are also Chittagong-Jessore and Chittagong-Khulna flights.

Biman offices are located in:

Chittagong
Jasmine Palace, Mir Ahmed Sharak Rd, tel 86179

Comilla
Laksham Rd, Kotwali, tel 2341
Cox's Bazar
Room 4, Hotel Sayeman or Cox's Bazar Airport, tel 6
Dacca
100 Motijheel Commercial Area, tel 252321
Ishurdi
Masjid Building, West Tengri, tel 339
Jessore
Green Villa, tel 5023
Khulna
KDA Building, Old Jessore Rd, tel 4411
Pabna
Muktha Mahal, Radha Nagar, tel 6290
Rajshahi
Sagarpara Rd, Ghoramora, tel 2193
Syedpur
TR Rd, tel 2551
Sylhet
Shah Jallal Rd, tel 2110

RIVER

This is the traditional means of transport in a country that has 8000 km of navigable riverway. Water transport is mainly operated by the Bangladesh Inland Waterway Transport Corporation (BIWTC), which runs a ferry and launch service on the main routes. There are also launch and ferry services run by private companies.

Besides the main ferry services between Dacca, Barisal and Khulna, and launch service between Narayanganj and Munshinganj, the BIWTC operates 'Rocket' ferries, launches and sea trucks on the following routes:

Kumira-Guptachara (East Sondwip)
Chittagong-Kutubdia
Chittagong-Hatiya
Chittagong-Barisal via Sondwip and Hatiya
Barghuna-Patarghata
Cox's Bazar-Maheshkali
Hatiya-Changobar
Hatiya-Charchuga

Patuakhali-Amtole
Patuakhali-Khupupera

See the relevant sections for schedules and fares.

Travelling on the riverboats is a high point of a visit to Bangladesh for many travellers. One visitor's report on the Chittagong-Barisal trip, travelling Inter-class:

.... We slept in one of the lifeboats. Quite comfortable. Fantastic night sky, millions of stars. The people on the boat were very friendly. We were given cups of tea and the cook gave us food to sample as they were preparing it. Very curious people, they do not see many tourists. Meals were very good – rice, chicken, dhal, vegetables, salad – and big helpings.
Mark Dwyer.

And a report on the Khulna-Dacca trip, travelling 1st class:

The Khulna-Dacca 'Rocket' service was wonderful. First class cabins have two berths, fans, sink, wood panelling and clean common toilets and showers for 1st class only. The whole front half of the upper deck of the old paddlewheel steamers is reserved for 1st class passengers. You can sit in big chairs and have the stewards serve tea and biscuits as you cruise the Ganges delta. Meals are extra but are reasonable (about Tk 20) and are served in the pleasant 1st class mess.

If you are leaving from Khulna you should be allowed to sleep the night before in your cabin, departure is at dawn. They move the boat to a different anchorage for the night so get aboard early. Then in the morning the boat sails back to the loading dock. Second class and deck class is fairly crowded and gross, but possible if you are shoestringing.

In Dacca 'Rocket' tickets are available from the BIWTC office, upstairs in the building across from the main Biman office. Try to book in advance, 1st class is popular. Travelling overland between Calcutta and Dacca the Khulna-Dacca 'Rocket' service is a great way to

Passenger Launch, Munshinganj

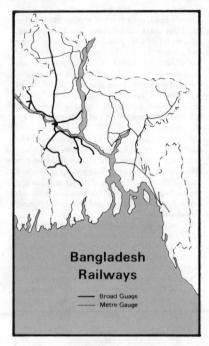

Bangladesh Railways

—— Broad Guage
—— Metre Gauge

make the trip. You can travel from Jessore to Khulna by bus.

Tom Harriman & Jan King

RAIL

There is about 2800 km of train track, a mixture of broad gauge west of the Brahmaputra (Jamuna) River and narrow gauge to the east. The Jamuna and the Meghna are both bridged.

Train travel is not like that experienced in India and Pakistan; it is not as crowded and the locals tend to be a bit more sociable. It also seems the locals hardly know the difference between 1st, 2nd and 3rd class. If they're discovered travelling in one of the upper classes they're simply left to stay where they are – quite a different situation from what happens in India! If the country was a little less destitute treatment of the poor probably wouldn't be as humane. On the narrow gauge trains 2nd and 3rd class seats are both benches arranged lengthwise; the only difference is that the 2nd class ones are padded.

Chiliharti, the northern border point, is linked with Khulna in the south. The narrow gauge track from the Dacca Division extends over into Rajshahi where it splits off in several directions: Rangpur, Dinajpur, Bogra, and to the east into the Chittagong Division where it splits again to Chittagong in the south and Sylhet in the north.

For specific schedules and fares check the relevant sections. Because of the many rivers some railway routes can be very roundabout. Between any two cities the difference in distance to be travelled by road, rail or river can be quite different.

Concessions

No concessions are offered to tourists, students or tour groups on planes, ferries or buses. These groups are given concessions on trains in 1st-class and 1st-class-airconditioned compartments. The concession varies according to the category: students 50%, others 25%.

Apply at the office of the Commercial Manager or the Divisional Railway Officer in Dacca or Chittagong. In Dacca the office is in the Railway Annex building in the Kamalapur area.

ROAD

Bangladesh has 6000 km of major roads, 4000 km of which is surfaced. At rivers the crossings are often made by ferries. Generally the roadways are poorly maintained and in disrepair. This is in some ways a blessing, as the innumerable potholes and dangerous shoulders prohibit any possibility of speeding. National highways are very narrow and double lanes for overtaking are virtually unheard of; to overtake, or sometimes to just pass one of the vehicles involved has to pull right off the road.

Like India's, Bangladesh's road transport fleet is a potpourri of vehicles. Minibuses and large public buses dominate; neither have much legroom. Although the express buses sometimes have bigger seats they still tend to be short of legroom for the average westerner. Night express buses often have television and cassette players, which are usually in a similar condition to the roads.

Longer distance bus services start generally at 5.30 am and go to 3 pm, and then re-start at 8.30 till 10.30 pm. There is often no time difference between express and ordinary buses because they also make frequent stops to pick up passengers. Express buses are, sometimes, more discriminating over whom they pick up, however!

Owner-drivers

The import of a vehicle requires the possession of a *carnet de passage* with registration in the home country and on the condition it is taken out of the country.

The *Automobile Association of Bangladesh* (tel 402241) can be contacted in Dacca at 3/B Lower Circular Rd, Mogh Bazar.

Car Rental

There are car-hire agencies in Dacca and Chittagong, mainly run by Parjatan Tourist Information Centres. The large hotels also house private agencies with similar rates to those at Parjatan. A car or jeep is Tk 40 per hour plus Tk 5 per km.

LOCAL TRANSPORT

There is the usual assortment of buses, taxis with meters that have never worked, autorickshaws (babytaxis) and rickshaws. Bus fares are very low, taxi and babytaxi fares are determined by time and distance.

Within the Dacca city perimeter a taxi fare is usually Tk 60, while for an babytaxi it's Tk 15. Taxis are usually black-yellow and pretty drab. Rickshaws usually charge Tk 1 per km. In contrast with the taxis they are the most ornately decorated contraptions on the streets of Bangladesh – garishly painted and decorated with pictures of cinema stars and hung with tinsel. At night they have little lanterns hanging below the seats.

The main problem with using urban public transport – buses – in Bangladesh is that all their destination signs are in Bengali script, quite indecipherable to most Europeans. Plus, of course, they are impossibly crowded.

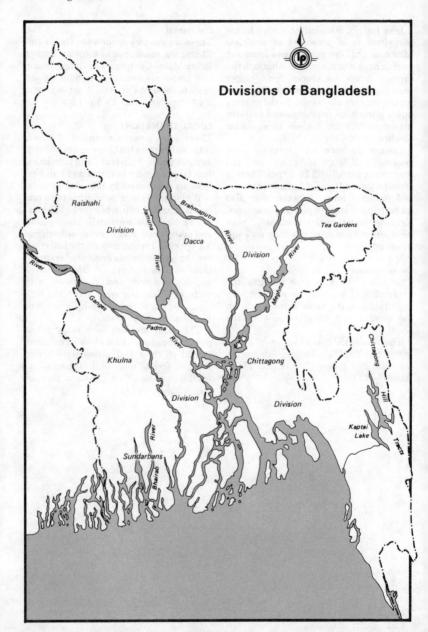

Divisions of Bangladesh

Dacca Division

Dacca is also spelt Dhaka. For consistency all references to the division, district or city of Dacca or to hotel or other names incorporating the word Dacca are always spelt 'Dacca' in this book, irrespective of the actual spelling in Bangladesh.

Dacca Division is located in the middle of the country and is surrounded to the west, south, and east by the three other administrative regions with the Indian border to the north. It consists of the districts of Jamalpur, Mymensingh, Tangail, Dacca and Faridpur, all bounded, except for the last, by the great rivers the Jamuna, the Padma and the Meghna.

In the northern district of Mymensingh the Garo Hills rise to a maximum of 240 metres; below these are forested swamplands called *haor* which abound with wildlife; from here the topography flattens to the south towards Madhupur. To the east and west the division tends to be dry with sandy alluvial plains. South of the district of Dacca the estuarine delta influence begins to carve up the landscape. It is this region of the division that is so often the victim of floods caused by tropical cyclones, like the disastrous

storm of mid-85. These natural disasters can summon up six-metre waves which devastate villages and crops and lead to the spread of disease.

The tropical climate makes this region warm, rainy and humid till October, and cool from November to March. With nearly 28 million people it is also the most densely populated division of the country.

There are no traces of early settlement in the region apart from the southern region, around Savar and Vikrampur, where there have been discoveries of ancient Buddhist settlements. They are of a much later period than those found in Rajshahi and Comilla districts, but not of such quality. It was in this region that the old Buddhist settlements eventually developed into major cities. When overland trade declined and the emphasis shifted to the coast the Dacca region overshadowed the ancient capital of Gaur.

Muslim rule was established in northern Bengal in 1204 and the Hindu Senas fled south and settled in Vikrampur till 1242. Rivalry with the fellow Hindu Devas in Sonargaon weakened their resistance against the Muslim onslaughts and in

45

1278 Vikrampur fell. Sonargaon lasted another decade and continued as a subsidiary capital with Gaur as the principal capital city.

In 1338 the Sultanate of Bangala was established and as maritime trade with South-East Asia flourished Sonargaon finally became the capital of the sultanate. It became known as Hazrat Jallal Sonargaon or the 'Seat of the Mighty Majesty'. The city stretched for 60 km by 30 km at the confluence of the Meghna, Brahmaputra and Lakhya rivers and was described by Mu Huang as enclosed with high walls and with broad streets, mosques, bazars and temples. It was guarded by the forts of Dur-duriya on the banks of the Bonar river and the Egarasindur fort on the north-east of the junction of the Bonar and Brahmaputra rivers. Only traces of ruins of this extensive city now remain.

Early in the 17th century the Sultanate of Bangala collapsed under pressure from the Moghuls. Sonargaon fell in 1611 but it appeared too exposed to attacks and Dacca was chosen as the site of the new capital. In 1757 the whole of Bangala fell into the hands of the British. With the exception of Dacca, the Moghul rulers never attached much importance to this region. Nor did the British during their period of rule show any particular interest in developing it. That is, until jute became a commercially valuable commodity and the northern district of Mymensingh became the centre for growing this 'golden fibre'.

DACCA

The evolution of the city of Dacca can be divided into four periods: the pre-Moghul stage, dominated by Buddhists and Hindus to the 13th century; the Muslim period of the Moghul Empire; the British rule; and the Pakistan and independence period.

First settled in the 4th century, Dacca's initial period of glory came with the Moghuls who utilised its strategic position over the Bay of Bengal and as a trading base. Dacca became the capital of the region after Sonargaon fell to the Moghuls in 1611.

Dacca first received principal status in 1608 when the Moghuls established their capital there. It was then called Jahangir Nagar; however, the first Moghul viceroy, so the story goes, was greeted by a chorus of drums, either warning outlying villages or welcoming him. This so impressed him that he ordered the region within earshot of the drums to be called Dhaka, from the Bengali word *dhak* meaning drum. An alternative version is that the city was named after the Hindu goddess Dhakeswari.

Dacca became the chief commercial emporium of the Moghuls, so much so that forts were built along the river banks to protect the city from Portuguese and Mogh pirates. In 1626 the Mogh pirates and their Portuguese allies briefly took Dacca and in 1639 the capital was moved to Rajmahal until 1659, leaving Dacca merely as the administrative centre. This had the effect of encouraging a greater concentration of commerce; maritime trade brought with it industry, Islamic education and a flourish of social life. As many as 100 vessels annually arrived to unload their cargo in Narayanganj and to load up with rice, sugar, fats, oilseeds and wax. Exotic goods were imported from Central Asia, Persia, Afghanistan and Turkey and the influx of foreign money resulted in cowrie shells being replaced with silver as the local currency.

Dacca remained the capital under the Moghuls until 1704 when they moved it to Murshidabad. Under the control of the Moghuls Dacca was considerably enhanced; they built mosques, palaces, caravanserais, bazars and gardens. This development began to attract European traders from southern India. Five Augustinians led by Father Bernard de Jesus arrived in Dacca in 1599 and established the first Christian mission here. In 1616 it became their official missionary centre for the region. They were followed by Portuguese traders who were given the area of Ichamata, about 18 km from the city centre, now called Ferringi Bazar. Some of these traders entered the service of the Moghuls.

They were soon followed by the Dutch who established their trading posts in Dholai Khal, a more favoured place, right in the centre of the commercial area. In 1682 the French arrived and like the Dutch sided with the Moghuls against the Portuguese and Mogh pirates. Tejgaon, the area north of Dholai Khal, was assigned to the Europeans by the Moghuls and it was in this section of the city where they had their headquarters, residences and churches.

The Church of Our Lady of the Holy Rosary was built here by the Portuguese in 1677, it's the oldest church in Bangladesh. The European communities, the Portuguese, the Dutch and the French were all at loggerheads with one another in their rivalry and competition for the favours of the Moghuls. The Armenians and some Greeks also arrived on the scene but they settled around the peripheral area south of Tejgaon where the 1781 Armenian Church of the Holy Resurrection still stands.

Like the Greeks the Armenians concentrated on inland trade but it was the Armenians who pioneered the jute trade in the second half of the 19th century until they were overrun by the British monopolies. The first Englishman to arrive in Dacca was one James Hart who arrived in 1658. In 1666 the East India Company established a trading post in Dacca but fell afoul of the Moghul viceroy, Shaista Khan. Dacca's decline as a maritime trade centre had already begun, however, as Narayanganj began to lose ground to the new port of Satgaon, later to become Calcutta.

The East India Company had extended their power so far that by 1757 they controlled all of Bangala although it was not until 1765 that they took over Dacca. The Moghul Nawab of Bangala, Naim Nizamat, was allowed to govern under the British. Not until 1824 did they take over

direct control and administration of the city. It was under their auspices that the dominant forms of economic development that remain today were established: vast plantations of indigo, sugar, tobacco, tea and, of course, jute. At the same time the other European powers were eased out; the Dutch surrendered their property to the British in 1781.

Apart from a few sufi and fakir-led uprisings, easily put down by the British, the 1800s passed fairly uneventfully, reflecting the growing consolidation of British rule on the subcontinent. In 1887 Dacca finally became a district and in 1905 Bengal was divided into two districts, East and West, the eastern section incorporating Assam with Dacca as its capital. From this point on, Dacca began to assume some measure of importance as an administrative centre. Government buildings, churches, residential enclaves and educational institutions transformed it into a city of prosperity. The partition of Bengal into East and West was undone in 1912 but Dacca remained the unofficial capital of the eastern portion and naturally became the capital of East Pakistan at the time of partition.

During the existence of East Pakistan, Dacca was classed as a subsidiary capital. It was not until independence in 1971 that Dacca once again achieved capital status in its own right. From a population of less than two million in 1971 Dacca has exploded to around five million today.

Information

The Parjatan Tourist Information Centre (tel 509479, 252911) is located in the Dacca Sheraton, at the intersection of Minto Rd and Mymensingh Rd. There is another office at Zia International Airport while the head office is at the Old Airport Building, Airport Rd.

The Archaeology Department (tel 327608) is at 22/1 Babur Rd, Mohammedpur. Entry is via Azad Gate and the archaeology library is within walking distance on the same road.

Banks
American Express (tel 283173-93), Motijheel Commercial Area, open 9 am to 1 pm daily, 9 to 11 am Fridays, closed Sundays. There is also a branch office at Hotel Sonargaon.
Chartered Bank (tel 251372-46), Motijheel Commercial Area, has similar hours to American Express.
Grindlay's Bank (tel 246812-14), Dilkusha Rd, Motijheel Commercial Area, similar hours.
Sonali Bank (tel 252990-99), Motijheel Commercial Area.

Other local banks, like those at the Hotel Sonargaon, are open from 9 am to 4 pm; 9 am to 1 pm Fridays. The Dacca Sheraton foreign exchange bank is open only to resident guests. You can do about 20% better than the bank rate at shops in various locations in Dacca, particularly around major hotels.

Post & Telegraph The General Post Office is near the Baitul Moharram Mosque on Abdul Gani Rd just off Bangbandhu Avenue. To find poste restante you have to turn right off the central hall and go down the corridor then left into a narrow passageway. There is another post office on Shahabaoh Ripon Rd near the National Museum which is open from 8 am to 8.30 pm.

The Central Telegraph Office is just a block from the GPO on the right just before the Fulbaria Central Bus Terminal.

Photographics Several photo studios do processing in 24 hours for Tk 30. Colour prints are Tk 8-10 per copy. The Dacca Sheraton seems to be the only place with Kodachrome or Ektachrome film for sale (Tk 400).

There is a camera repair shop, Haque Sans, which offers 24-hour service, on Airport Rd, just a short distance to the north of Farm Gate on the right. It's not easy to find as it is located down a narrow lane. The service charge is usually Tk 40.

Shopping Most international hotels have shopping arcades and handicraft centres. Other individual centres are Stadium Arcade, New Market, Chandni Chowk Bazar, Paltan Super Market, Palwell Shopping Centre and the Gulshan Supermarket.

There is an Export Promotion Bureau just opposite the Dacca Sheraton on Mymensingh Rd. It has a wide range of excellent quality selections from leatherwork, woodcarving, jute products, textiles, garments, silk and cotton, artwork and carpets. All payments have to be made in foreign currency.

The Karika Handicraft Emporium is also opposite the Dacca Sheraton. It also has on display jute products like doormats and carpets, wall pieces, bronze work, leatherwork, purses and handbags, garments and jewellery. They accept takkas here.

Bangladesh Handicrafts (tel 403449) is at 68 Outer Circular Rd on Mogh Bazar. The Sericulture Display Centre at 140 Jakanara Garden, Green Rd has silk saris and finished silken garments on display, both block-printed and embroidered.

East-West Handicrafts (tel 316946), Rd No 6, House 17, Mirpur Rd, Dhanmondi Residential Area has handicrafts including clothing, dolls, ceramic vases, woodwork, handbags made of bamboo, jute and leather, table pieces, embroidered quilts and also artwork including paintings and sculptural pieces.

For jewellery try Chandan in the DIT Supermarket, Mymensingh Rd or Pearls Paradise at 20 Baitul Moharram. The Jazni Display Centre at 224/1 New Eskaton Rd has shell crafts. For jute carpets there's the Baghdad-Dacca Carpet Factory at the Hotel Sonargaon. Boutiques include Silk House at the Dacca Sheraton and Women's Paradise at G-2 North DIT Supermarket in Gulshan. Finally the Dacca Warehouse, KDC Guesthouse, No 3, Rd No 11, Gulshan 2, sells liquor and cigarettes, but apparently only to VIPs and aid personnel.

Top: Istara Mosque, Dacca (JRS)
Bottom: Pari Bibi Mausoleum, Dacca (JRS)

Top: Dhakeswari Temple, Dacca (BPC)
Bottom: Sat Gombad Mosque, Dacca (BPC)

Art Galleries
Bangladesh Shilpakala Academy, Segunbagicha.
Bangladesh College of Arts & Crafts, Mymensingh Rd.
Contemporary Art Ensemble (tel 302266), 48/1 Commercial Building, South Avenue, Gulshan.
Jiraj Art Gallery, Shahbagh Shopping Arcade.
Tivoli Art Gallery (tel 301847), F-33 Gulshan, DIT Supermarket, Gulshan.
Hoque Handicrafts, F-43 Gulshan 2, DIT Supermarket, Gulshan.
Saju Arts & Crafts (tel 302513), F-18-38 Gulshan, DIT Supermarket, Gulshan.

Libraries
British Council Library, near the University of Dacca.
American Centre, No 8 Rd, No 9 Dhanmondi Area.
Alliance Francaise Library.
Dacca University Library.
Dacca Public Library, Mymensingh Rd, near the National Library.

Swimming Pools Non-guests can use the pools at the Sonargaon Hotel or the Dacca Sheraton for Tk 40.

Things to See
Dacca is a fairly large and sprawling city. It is dotted with over 700 mosques, all equipped with PA systems to let the faithful know when prayer time is upon them; there are 18 public parks which offer pleasant respite from the constant bustle, but, alas, at last count only seven public urinals, so plan your day carefully.

The city of Dacca can be roughly divided into three sections, each defined by the period of colonial occupation that gave rise to its architecture.

Old City
The oldest and most southerly section of the city runs along the north bank of the waterfront region. It emerged during the time when Dacca was a significant Moghul trading centre of the empire. Dholai Khal was the first site of the Moghul city and is today the oldest part of Dacca, about eight km above the Buriganga confluence with

the Dhakeswari, where the ghats are located. Immediately above the ghats are the bazars around which the Europeans formerly had their trading posts.

The waterfront is always a frenzy of activity at the two main water transport terminals, Saddarghat and Badam Tole. Both these are located along the Buckland Rd Bund, which runs the length of the waterfront.

Saddarghat & Badam Tole This area is always crowded with people and thronged with watercraft of all types. Badam Tole, where the BIWTC 'Rocket' ferries dock, is west along the Buckland Bund Rd. Between the two is the **Ahsan Manzil**, the old baroque-style palace of the last Nawab of Dacca, Naim Nizamat. It remains imposing with its grand stairways and large state rooms but is now in disrepair and has become a slum habitation; even the roof has been built over with shanties.

An ancient cannon stands on the Saddarghat. It's said to be a male gun, known as Kale Jham Jham, and its female mate, Bibi Mariam, is somewhere at the bottom of the river. The curious booming noise known as the Barisal guns which is sometimes heard at night is Bibi Mariam calling to Kale Jham Jham.

The panorama of riverlife on the Buriganga is particularly fascinating here. You can hire boats to explore the river from here for Tk 20 to 30 per hour. A little further west are the mid-17th century **Bara Katra** and **Chotta Katra**; the former apparently meant to be a palace or residence and the latter a caravanserai for visiting merchants. It was originally quadrangular with 22 rooms around a central courtyard with gates to the north and south. Above the Bund is Islampur Rd which ends to the west on Bangla Bazar, from where another road continues and terminates at the Lalbagh Fort area. The area around the Lalbagh Fort is filled with labyrinthine laneways which meander past ancient and medieval buildings.

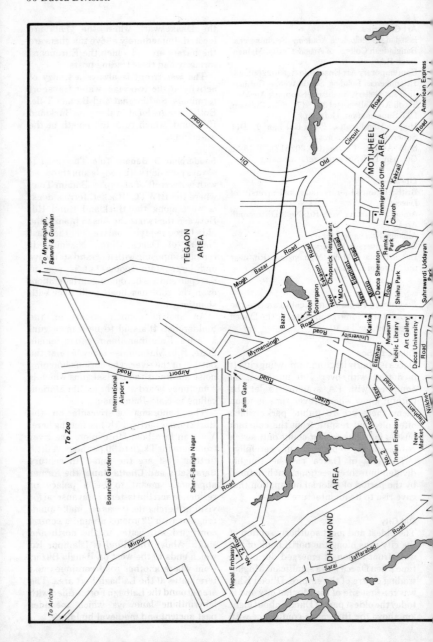

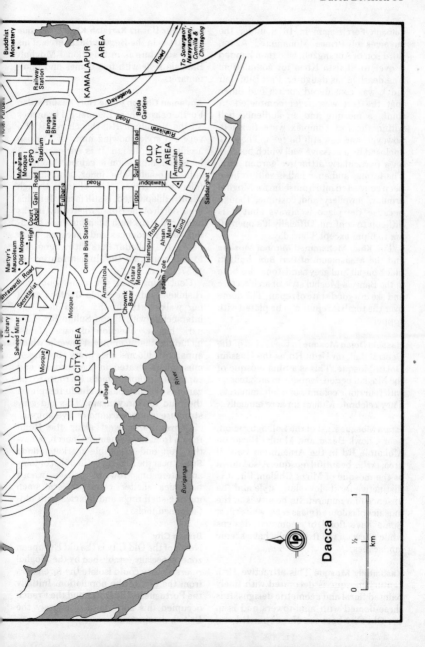

Lalbagh Fort Begun in 1678 under the auspices of Prince Mohammed Azam, third son of Aurangzeb, who then handed it over to Shaista Khan for completion. The death of his daughter, Pari Bibi (fair lady), was considered such a bad omen that the fort was never completed. A tomb, a mosque and an audience hall within the fort complex were finished, however, and can still be seen. They are enclosed by a massive wall which borders on a particularly attractive garden area. The former audience hall is said to have been converted into a museum for Moghul armour, jewellery and costume, though because the place is always shut it is difficult to confirm. Officially it's open 10 am to 6 pm except Thursdays.

The **Khan Mohammed Mirdhai Mosque** and the **Mausoleum of Pari Bibi**, built in black basalt and grey sandstone, are both in the Bangala-Moghul style of architecture and are in a good state of repair. The dome over the tomb is reputed to be plated with copper.

Hassain Dolan Mosque In the region of the Central Jail, on Urdu Rd, is the Hassain Dolan Mosque. This is a Shia mosque of the Moghul period, baroque in architecture with four doric columns and four minarets. They celebrate Muharram here annually.

Istara Mosque East of the Lalbagh region, near Chowk Bazar and Moulvi Bazar on Mohatole Rd in the Armanitola Patuali area, is this beautiful mosque. Also known as the mosque of Mirza Ghulam Pir, it is distinctive for its low-slung style and the absence of a minaret. Its beauty is in the mosaics of coloured glass set in white tiles. Some have floral or geometric designs while a few on the front walls have scenic landscapes.

Kashaitully Mosque This attractive 19th century mosque is decorated with finely painted floral and geometric designs. It is three-domed with mini-towers and is in the Old City between Nawabpur Rd and Islampur Bazar. **Kartalab Khan's Mosque** of 1704 is in the Begum Bazar area. This large structure is in traditional Moghul-Bangala style with five domes and mini-minarets.

Armenian Church of the Holy Resurrection Further east, where Liaquat Rd branches off the Nawabpur Rd, this church is of a very old style showing hints of Turkish architectural design. It is enclosed by a high wall; admission is gained through a side ante-hall. The inner courtyard is filled with graves. The church, though slightly dilapidated, is still in use. It is this area, north of the Bund, where the Greeks and Armenians built their business head-quarters, residences and churches. Near here is the Bahadur Park with a cenotaph to commemorate the 'Indian Mutiny' of 1857.

Continuing west you come onto the Rishikesh Rd. The **Balda Gardens** are a fair walk north on this road near the intersection with Tippu Sultan Rd. This park has a collection of rare plants, including the 'Century Flower', which apparently blooms once every 16 years. A museum is located in the gardens and contains Moghul artifacts. En route to the gardens you may pass a Hindu temple on the road to Narayanganj. This old grey structure is *pancharatma* or five-spired.

Chowk Bazar, west along the Bund region from the Armenian Church, is now the fruit and vegetable market. **Hindu Street**, near the Armenian Church, contains an interesting row of houses whose balconies shelter countless craftsmen making shell rings and bangles with old-fashioned tools.

British City
North of the Old City is the old European zone, especially established by the Moghul rulers so they could isolate the foreigners from the rest of the population. Initially the Portuguese, the Dutch and the French occupied this zone until ultimately the British dominated.

The British, as with everywhere in the subcontinent, left their mark principally in the institutions they established. In the Ramna area, where they concentrated, is the administrative and social panoply of British rule: the Secretariat, Dacca College, the governor's residence (now the Supreme Court) and Curzon Hall.

This central region of the city contains most of the modern public institutions. The **Banga Bhavan**, the official residence of the president, is just one block away from the Fulbaria bus terminal. Photography, even of the gate, is forbidden. Dacca University, the Public Library and Museum are all near the old British zone which ultimately extended up to the Dhanmondi area and Mogh Bazar in the north-west. The Dhanmondi area, while fairly modern, contains the **New Market** and a number of ancient monuments and relics. The best of these is the **Idgah**, a Moghul remnant dating from about 1640 and consisting of a five-metre-high structure with carved stone screen walls and an octagonal central mihrab.

The British zone is also where the stadium, the GPO and the Baitul Moharram Mosque are located. Also, near the Sheraton Hotel are the **Suhrawardi Uddayan** gardens (formerly known as the Race Course) where both the Bangladeshi declaration of independence and the surrender of Pakistani occupation forces took place in 1971. At the northern end is the **Shishu Park** amusement centre for children. Adjacent to this is the **Ramna Garden Park** with a boating lake.

At the southern end of the park is the High Court, close to the newly constructed **Mausoleum for Three Martyrs**. Very close to this is the **Mazhar & Mosque of Haji Khwaja Shahbaz** which dates from 1679. Off Secretariat Rd is the **Central Shaheed Minar** near the Dacca College of Medicine. It has a hangman's scaffold design in memory of the martyrs of the 1952 Language Movement.

In the same area is the British Council Library and immediately north of the university are the College of Arts & Crafts which has an art gallery, the Dacca Public Library and the National Museum, which has an attractive modern design. The **National Museum** houses a collection that ranges from the Hindu and Buddhist eras through to the Moghul period. It consists of sculptural works, engravings, terracotta friezes, miniature paintings, ancient manuscripts, coins, pottery, ivory and silver filigree work. The museum is open 10 am to 4 pm except on Friday when it is open 3 to 7 pm and Thursday when it is closed. To the north is Dhakeswari Rd where the **Dhakeswari Temple** is near the Engineering University. It's design is peculiar to Dacca.

Past the Dacca Sheraton on Minto Rd is the fortress-like **State Guest House** complete with guard towers. Northward is the Mogh Bazar and on Mymensingh Rd the Sonargaon Hotel. At Farm Gate the Mymensingh Rd splits into Airport Rd and the Mirpur Rd which passes through Sher-e-Bangla en route to the zoo and botanical gardens. The Airport Rd passes Mohakhali, Tejgaon and the Banani Model Town. East of Banani is another model town, the Gulshan Residential Area, the most expensive area of Dacca.

South of Gulshan and east of Purana Paltan is the Motijheel Commercial Area, dominated by the Central Bank Building. This is also where the Purbani Hotel, the American Express office, the US Embassy and various bank offices are located. To the east is the Central Railway Station and beyond, a short distance from the railway tracks, is the **Dharmarajikha Buddhist Monastery**.

Modern City

Further north, the 20th century is most evident in Banani, the diplomatic enclave, and the Gulshan Commercial Area, the 'Garden City' of the rich. The Motijheel Commercial Area, in the east, is where all the modern trappings of city life are to be found: hotels, banks, restaurants, travel agencies and big businesses.

Sher-E-Bangla Nagar, north of the Dhanmondi area, is where the National Assembly building, the **Gana Bhavan,** is located. This is one of the most modern areas of Dacca. Just behind is the modern **Dacca Exhibition Fair.** West of Sher-e-Bangla is Muhammadpur. The **Sat Gombad Mosque,** another Moghul seven-domed mosque built in the 17th century, is located at the end of the road to Sarai Jafarabad. This is the limit of the Moghul city on this side of Dacca.

Suburban Dacca

Mirpur Zoo To get to the zoo take a minibus from Farm Gate at the end of Mymensingh Rd. The route does not, unfortunately, run directly to the zoo, but stops short by two km. Remind the bus conductor of your destination before you're too far out. From the drop-off point (Tk 2 fare), take a rickshaw, which should cost about Tk 3. Entrance to the zoo is Tk 2.

The grounds of the zoo are set around two lakes which serve as a sanctuary for migratory birdlife, mostly ducks. This is probably the best place to get a look at the indigenous flora and fauna of Bangladesh if you don't have time to flush it out for yourself in the provinces.

Botanical Gardens East of the zoo the gardens contain over one thousand species of local and foreign tropical and sub-tropical plants.

Outside Dacca The delta region begins immediately south of Dholai Khal while 16 km north-west in the area of Kurmitola the Bhawal jungle begins and spreads north for over 160 km towards Tangail.

The southern banks of the Buriganga is now made up of villages with dry-docking and boat-building yards. West of this area is mainly villages and four km further up from Dholai Khal is a bamboo suspension bridge. To the east are brick kilns with smokestacks rising above the landscape. Ghats on the southern bank are minor

affairs – it's on the north bank you find the Badam Tole Ghat and Saddarghat as well as other important ghats like Dabidas Ghat, Savari Ghat and Wise Ghat. The minor ghats are generally market places where boats laden with produce unload.

City Tours

The Parjatan Tourist Information Centre (tel 252911) in the Dacca Sheraton rents cars and jeeps for city tours. Rates are Tk 40 per hour plus Tk 5 per mile. They also have minibuses available at Tk 60 per hour plus Tk 6 per mile. Parjatan also hire speedboats for Tk 250 per hour. Other car-hire agencies can be found in other large hotels. Dacca Tour Rent-A-Car Association (tel 282215) is on Minto Rd.

Parjatan also has guided tours of the city, the suburbs and outlying districts. They require a group of at least 10 for a minibus, at least 15 for a larger aircon bus. Tours include:

Tour 1 Old City, Saddar area, British enclave, modern city, monuments, etc. Tours are 8 am to 12 noon and 1 to 5 pm during the summer season and cost Tk 50.
Tour 2 Covers the Zoo and Botanical Garden and operates at the same time and for the same fare as Tour 1.
Suburban Tour Goes to Narayanganj and Sonargaon and costs Tk 60 or Tk 75 in an aircon bus, including a soft drink or cup of tea!
Outlying Area Tour 1 Goes to the Pajendrapur National Park and costs Tk 65 or Tk 80 in an aircon bus. Lunch costs an additional Tk 100.
Outlying Area Tour 2 This tour goes to Mainimati, 104 km east of Dacca, and costs Tk 150 or Tk 200 in an aircon bus. Again lunch is an additional Tk 100.

You can hire taxis and babytaxis by the hour at a cost of about Tk 60 per hour plus Tk 5 per mile for a taxi, Tk 30 plus Tk 2.50 for a babytaxi.

If you want to take yourself on a tour by the sweat of somebody else's brow, you can hire a rickshaw and navigate your way around. The going rate is Tk 3-4 per km or Tk 15 per hour. Don't stay with the same driver for the whole tour as they tend to slow down to prolong the journey (they may just be getting tired, of course). Don't take rickshaws from outside an international hotel as they have been known to charge the more affluent members of the tourist fraternity Tk 40 per hour. Fix a rate before you begin to avoid any hassles. Drivers tend to attract a supportive crowd if they get into a squabble with tourists. Alternatively, if you think your driver has served you well, a Tk 2 tip is considered enough.

Places to Stay – bottom end

Hotel Asia (tel 281859) on Top Khana Rd is cheap, clean and friendly with shared bathroom singles/doubles at Tk 45/55. The *Ambassador Hotel*, on Mymensingh Rd opposite the Arab-Bangladesh Bank, offers singles/doubles at Tk 40/65. *Hotel Noor* at 26 Green Rd in the Dhanmondi Area, has rooms with attached bath, fans and mosquito nets for Tk 45/80.

Hotel Titas (tel 401891), 246 Circular Rd, Mogh Bazar has rooms with shared or attached bath, with fans and mosquito nets. Singles are Tk 35, doubles Tk 50, triples Tk 90 or Tk 60 with shared bathroom. The *Shabeekha Hotel* at the corner of Circular Rd and Mogh Bazar also has rooms with common or attached bath. Singles are Tk 35, doubles Tk 60, quadruples Tk 120.

Right at the bottom of the bottom end are places like the *Grand Hotel* on Mymensingh Rd in a bazar two blocks north of the expensive Hotel Sonargaon. The rooms are very basic and a little grotty – singles/doubles are Tk 30/50. The *Hotel du Prince* is down an alley in the Saddarghat area and again is a pretty basic place intended for local travellers. Triples are Tk 60. *Hotel Al Fatah*, 158 Nawabpur Rd, Old City Area, is a boarding house with rooms with common bath at Tk 20/32. *Hotel Sharif* at 3 Hassanullah Rd in the old city area of Islampur also has basic rooms at Tk 20/30.

Finally in the Kamalapur area, within walking distance to the north-east of the Central Railway Station, there's a *Buddhist Monastery* where it may be possible to stay. You have to apply to the head monk for permission; it's usually free but, of course, a small present is expected.

Places to Stay – middle

Lord's Inn International is on New Eskaton Rd opposite the Chop Stick Restaurant. It's a new building with rooms with attached bath, fans and mosquito nets and prices of Tk 75/105. By now there should be a restaurant and snack bar. *Hotel Al-Helal*, Arambagh, Motijheel Commercial Area, has a restaurant and singles are Tk 65, doubles Tk 100, triples Tk 130.

Hotel Brighton (tel 312619-82) at 163 Elephant Rd in the Hatirpool area has singles at Tk 60, doubles Tk 100, triples Tk 130. The *Metropolitan Hotel* on North-South Rd is new and fairly clean with attached bath singles/doubles at Tk 75/125. *Hotel Rajdoot*, 24 Lower Circular Rd, has a restaurant and rooms at Tk 55/100.

The *Taj Hotel* on Nawabpur Rd in the old city is of a reasonable standard with singles/doubles at Tk 45/75. The *Al Sharif*, on Nawabpur Rd near the Gulistan Bazar, is similarly priced. The *Hotel Super*, between the Gulistan Bus Station and the Chittagong Bus Terminal, offers rooms at Tk 80 a double. It also has a good restaurant.

At the bottom of the middle bracket are places like the *Hotel Sat Tara* at 285 Mogh Bazar in an alley off and north of Circular Rd. It's fairly clean and quiet with rooms at Tk 40/75 or with attached bathroom at about 15% more. The *Hotel Aara* in the Farm Gate area has basic rooms with shared bath, fan and mosquito nets for Tk 40/80. At 86 Kakrail Rd the *Tourist Hotel* is clean, pleasant and modern. A double with bathroom, fan and mosquito nets is Tk 100.

The *YMCA Hostel* (hostel tel 307898, office tel 408204), 96/97 New Eskaton

Rd, has an annex hostel in an alley just across the road with dorm accommodation for Tk 40 a bed. The regular rooms have attached bath and cost Tk 70/100. Breakfast and lunch are available. A transient membership card will cost Tk 5 and is valid for three months. They also have a mail service here; enquire at the office. The YWCA hostel on Green Rd is now closed. On New Eskaton Rd near the YMCA the *Potenga Hotel* has rooms with and without bath from Tk 60 to 180.

Places to Stay – top end
Hotel Sonargaon (tel 315001-09), Kawran Bazar, Mymensingh Rd, is Dacca's number one hotel with all the usual trappings of international hotel life including restaurants, bar, discotheque, banks, cafe, lounge, conference rooms, shopping arcade, sauna, tennis courts, swimming pool, airline offices and an art gallery! You can pay from US$64 up to over US$400 for the most expensive suite.

The others of this ilk include the *Dacca Sheraton* (tel 252911-19) at the intersection of Minto Rd and Mymensingh Rd. It also has all the usual features (but no art gallery) and the Parjatan Tourist Office is located here. Rooms cost US$75 to 200 plus service charges. Third of Dacca's three top hotels is the *Hotel Purbani International* (tel 254081-85), 1 Dilkusha Rd, Motijheel Commercial Area, with rooms at Tk 600 to 1400.

The *Hotel Golden Gate* (tel 310321-5), 28 Mirpur Rd, near New Market, has aircon rooms from Tk 350 to 450. *Hotel Zakaria International* (tel 601172), 35 Gulshan Avenue, Mohakhali Commercial Area, has rooms from Tk 200 to 450.

Hotel Park International (tel 405791-92), 46 Kakrail Rd, has aircon rooms, a restaurant, tour agencies, laundry service and singles/doubles at Tk 280/350. The *Hotel Blue Nile* (tel 326400), 36 New Elephant Rd, has aircon rooms and in general is similar to the Park International. Singles are Tk 75-125, doubles Tk 150-250 and it's good value for money. The

City Hotel (tel 257905-06) at 21 Bongo Bandho Ave has TV, a pharmacy, aircon and prices from Tk 100 to 300.

Parjatan operate the *Airport Hotel* right at the airport. Singles cost Tk 180; when your Biman flight is cancelled this is where you'll stay.

Places to Eat
Cheap Eats *Super Duper Snack* on Mymensingh Rd, just around the corner of New Eskaton Rd, has a different menu every day, is fairly clean and serves mainly chicken, beef or mutton curries with rice, vegetables, salad and tea for Tk 16 and up.

The *New Al-Amin* is difficult to find: on Mymensingh Rd, similarly just around the corner of New Eskaton Rd but to the north and on the left side located within a courtyard. There's excellent biriyani here, and kebab and chicken tikka with nan. Again meals cost about Tk 16 and up.

In the Farm Gate area there are a number of similarly priced kebab and nan places although they are usually only open in the evenings. There are also local restaurants in the Mogh Bazar area with similar prices and standards. The rock bottom cheapies, where you can get a meal for Tk 2.50, are not recommended for hygienic reasons.

Mid-range Restaurants – Chinese Dacca has a surfeit of Chinese restaurants. Take your pick from any of these:

The *Tai King Restaurant*, on New Eskaton Rd, is run by locals but has a Chinese-trained cook. They compensate for quality with quantity. The *Shen Yang Restaurant*, just off Kakrail Rd, is a similar operation to the Tai King. The *Red Button Chinese Restaurant* and the *Tung Nan Chinese Restaurant* are both near Tejgaon on Airport Rd.

The *China Rose*, on Elephant Rd near the Hotel Brighton, is open only from 6 to 10.30 pm. Just behind the Ali Baba Specialized Restaurant, near the junction of Mymensingh Rd on University Rd in Paribagh, the *King Queen Chinese Restaurant* is open similar hours. Ditto for the *Golden Dragon Restaurant* at 242 Saddar Rd in the Mohakhali area, the *Hong Kong Chinese Restaurant* at 140 Gulshan Avenue in Gulshan, the *Taipan Chinese Restaurant* at 2/5 Mirpur Rd, and the *Shanghai* and *Nanking Chinese Restaurants*, both on Mirpur Rd.

The *Cathay Chinese Restaurant* at 1st DIT Supermarket in Gulshan, the *Mandarin Restaurant* at the corner of Purana Paltan and North-South Rd, and the *Cafe Canton* on Top Khana Rd are open from 11 am to 3 pm as well as the evening session.

The *Beijing Restaurant*, near the Blue Nile Hotel, has good food and service and is relatively cheap. The *Hwang Ho Restaurant*, Mymensingh Rd, opposite Super Duper Snack, is newly opened and has the same rates as any other Chinese restaurant in town.

Mid-range Restaurants – Local Food Apart from the purely local low price places there are a number of better places noted for their local food. The *Mary Anderson Floating Restaurant* is moored on the northern bank of the Buriganga in Pagla, eight km from the city, and is open 11 am to 3 pm, 6 to 9.30 pm. To get there take bus No 4 from the Central Bus Terminal at Fulbaria for the 20-minute trip. The restaurant is a large unused ferry run by the Parjatan Tourism Corporation. Prices are slightly higher than Chinese restaurants, but more than compensated for by the passing riverlife – little sampans, sailboats, launches, barges, ferries and so on. Across the river you can see brick kilns and heaped piles of freshly baked bricks. On the deck there are cane chairs and low tea-tables; it's a pleasant place to just sit and watch, quite apart from the food.

The *Darul Kebab Place* on Mymensingh Rd near the Ali Baba Specialized Restaurant does kebabs and chicken tikkas accompanied by wheat bread nan or chappatis; about Tk 20 a serve. *Sharif's Inn* on Toyonbee Rd offers local, western, and Chinese dishes and is reasonably priced, slightly lower than the Chinese restaurants.

There's also the *Bar-B-Q Hut* at 63 Block B, Road No 18, Banani which specialises in kebabs. Or try the *Cafe Grill* on Dilkusha Rd, Motijheel Commercial Area which has an excellent selection with meals from Tk 16 and up. The *YMCA Hostel* on New Eskaton Rd does a western breakfast for Tk 16, lunch is usually curry and rice and costs Tk 16, they don't serve dinner but they do snacks and tea.

Top End Restaurants Most of the large international hotels have restaurants which, of course, offer large-international-type cuisine. Several of them have excellent buffets.

The *Hotel Sonargaon Restaurant* does a buffet-style breakfast for Tk 110. You could eat enough here to last until dinner. At the *Dacca Sheraton* breakfast costs Tk 175, the bar opens at 6.30 pm, and the *Cafe Arami* is open around the clock – good for midnight snacks.

The *Chop Stick Restaurant*, New Eskaton Rd, is among the few Chinese restaurants actually managed by Chinese and is considered to be the best in town. The ice cream here is recommended. The *Ali Baba Specialised Restaurant*, on Mymensingh Rd across from the Sonargaon, is pricey but has excellent food. Their Ali Baba chicken is brought in sizzling on a mini-stove, like Japanese Sukiyaki. Meals generally cost Tk 90 to 100 plus tax. It's open from 11 am till 3 pm and from 6 to 10.30 pm.

The *Sakura Restaurant*, despite its name is not Japanese and in fact offers an eclectic choice of cuisine: Chinese, Japanese, Italian, French, and other western varieties. Alcohol is also available. The restaurant is on the 1st floor of the Karika Emporium near the Dacca Sheraton and is open 8 am to 10.30 pm. Prices are fairly reasonable.

Snacks Cheap places for a snack include the *Snack Bar* on New Eskaton Rd, a tiny saloon where you can get meat and vegetable rolls for Tk 2.50, hamburgers for Tk 6, coffee Tk 3, tea Tk 1. Try the *Rangoon Cafe* near New Market area for good lassi drinks. On New Eskaton Rd the *Ice Cream Parlour* is strictly stand up but their Tk 6 snacks and Tk 5 ice cream are excellent.

On Mymensingh Rd near New Eskaton Rd *Moslem Sweet Meats* is the place to try *mesti dhoi*, the unique Bangladesh dessert of yoghurt sweetened with brown sugar. There's a coffee bar across the road from the Blue Nile Hotel with good espresso coffee – and lousy fish and chips!

More expensive snack places include *Eva Snacks* on Dilkusha Rd near the Purbani International Hotel which is an excellent place for coffee and ice cream. The *Gourmet Shop* in the Dacca Sheraton has fine pastries and chocolate cakes.

Entertainment

The *American Marines Clubs* in the US Embassy compound in Gulshan Commercial Area has a disco every Friday from 9 pm to 3 am. You have to have your passport. Happy Hour is 8-9 pm. The Canadian Club, also on Gulshan Avenue, requires membership but you can be signed in temporarily by a member. There is also a disco at the *Dacca Sheraton* every Saturday night.

Membership is required at the *Dutch Recreation Club* in the Banani Area. There's also a British Aid Club at Rd No 43, House 35, Gulshan, which has a swimming pool but it's exclusively for diplomats and members of aid associations in Bangladesh.

Getting There & Away

Air Zia International Airport handles both international and domestic flights. If you fly out of Dacca make sure your luggage gets on the right trolley for the flight you are taking. The airline offices in Dacca are mainly in Motijheel Commercial Area:

Air India, Dacca Sheraton Hotel (tel 500070-71).
Bangladesh Biman Airlines, Biman Bhavan, Motijheel Commercial Area (tel 255911-35).
Burma Airways Corporation, Ramna Bhavan Rd, opposite City Hotel.
Indian Airlines, Purbani International Hotel (tel 231687).
Royal Nepal Airlines, Motijheel Commercial Area near Air India.
Thai International, Dacca Sheraton Hotel (tel 500074-9).

River BIWTC 'Rocket' ferries depart from Badam Tole Ghat. The better ferries are *MV Ghazi* and *MV Masood*; the *MV Tern* is definitely a second choice. These ply the Dacca-Barisal-Khulna route, taking about 24 hours. To make sure you get a decent berth, you can hire a boat from the dock to get out to the boat to stake a place on the deck before the hordes arrive. Others have been known to pay a local to occupy a place for them, sitting all day for a fee of Tk 7. Departure time is 6 pm; fares are 1st class Tk 424, 2nd class 257, Interclass Tk 124, deck class Tk 70.

For a comfortable and cheap trip on the 'Rockets', book a deck-class ticket, then rent a crew's berth for Tk 25 for the trip to Barisal, Tk 40-50 if you're going to Khulna. This is better than taking Interclass where there are only benches to sleep on, plus the strain of watching one's pack. However, if you do rent a crew berth, still chain your pack to the bed post or some such object – it's best to be on the safe side.

If you're on a really tight budget and can't even afford the crew berth, take yourself up to the 1st-class dining hall and sleep there. This is particularly useful in winter.

The alternative on the Dacca-Khulna route is the private launch *Maheskhali Steamer*. It's small but very cheap, departing 6 pm (get there by 3 pm to stake out a sleeping place) from the Saddarghat Launch Terminal. Fares are Tk 50 to Khulna, Tk 25 to Barisal.

Other launches operate along the coast

and to islands off the coast. Schedules and fares for these short distance services are very changeable. Short distance destinations reached by services from Dacca include:

Bandura: boats depart every half hour from 5.30 am till 3.30 pm. 1st class Tk 10, deck Tk 6.
Srinagar: same schedules and fares as Bandura.
Toltolla: schedule as above, 1st class Tk 15, deck Tk 8.

Longer routes from Dacca include:

Barisal: two medium-sized launches daily; depart 6 pm. 1st class Tk 150, deck Tk 20.
Bhula: two launches daily, depart 7 & 7.30 pm. 1st class Tk 150, deck Tk 20.
Patuakhali: two launches daily; depart 6 & 6.30 pm. 1st class Tk 150, deck Tk 20.
Madaripur: three launches daily at 8, 8.30, 9 pm. 1st class Tk 110, deck Tk 15.
Chandpur: two launches daily at 8 & 11 am. 1st class Tk 87, deck Tk 15.
SNB: three launches daily at 7, 8.30, 9 pm. 1st class Tk 60, deck Tk 15.
Khulna: one launch every alternate day at 6 pm. 1st class Tk 200, deck Tk 70.

Except for 1st class, bookings are usually on board the launches. There are no launches or ferries from Dacca or Chandpur to Chittagong.

Rail Trains are the most pervasive form of public transport in Bangladesh. They run to every major town and city in the country, are hardly ever on schedule, and travel slowly and often indirectly, especially the routes to Chittagong and Khulna.

For information on specific routes see the relevant sections. Discounts are offered to tourists, students and group tours.

The Central Railway Terminal building in Dacca is modern but not yet fully upgraded. There are hardly any signs in English, so you will have to ask around.

Road The Central Bus Station in Dacca is in Fulbaria on Station Rd. The road network in Bangladesh is well developed, and buses go to every town and village that a traveller could possibly wish to visit. Buses are also the cheapest, and hence most tiring, way of travelling through the countryside.

There are several bus terminals for different regions of the country. These have been set up to decongest the old Central Bus Station. The Mirpur Bus Terminal for the north-west and south-west regions (ie Rajshahi and Khulna) is about a km beyond the road to the zoo. To get there take the Savar bus from Fulbaria. The Gabtole Bus Terminal is for buses for Rangpur, Syedpur and Dinajpur. Buses to Rangpur cost Tk 76 and take about 10 hours.

The Moakhali Bus Terminal is for the northern regions like Tangail and Mymensingh. The Jatra Bari Bus Terminal on Narayanganj Rd is mainly for the eastern Chittagong Division, ie for Sylhet, Comilla, Chittagong and Cox's Bazar. Chittagong buses also go from the S A Paribahan Bus Agency near the Immigration Office. Deluxe buses cost Tk 65 and take seven hours overnight.

The Fulbaria Central Bus Terminal is mainly for city and suburban buses. For buses to Chittagong the departure point is, at least temporarily, the eastern gate of the Gulistan Bazar. The western gate is the location of ticket stalls and the buses for the north-west region such as Rajshahi, Rangpur and Bogra. The Fulbaria terminal has long outgrown its capacity so it seems rather chaotic, a situation not helped by the lack of signs in English script. Nevertheless, there are plenty of people to point you toward the right bus so it's no problem.

Getting Around

Airport Transport Despite the fact that there is no longer a curfew in major centres of Dacca (but there are still a few in some restricted military cantonments), it's best to arrive during the daytime: then there are no problems with taxis or babytaxis which both double their fares in the evening, nor with looking for a suitable hotel.

Taxi fare from Zia International airport is Tk 80; babytaxi Tk 40; minibus Tk 3; bus Tk 2.50. By bus the usual place to get off in the city is Farm Gate and then take a rickshaw (Tk 2-3) to a hotel.

There's a duty free shop at the airport where you can purchase duty free items including cigarettes, film and liquor before you pass through the immigration check point.

Bus & Ferry Stations The Central Bus Station is on Station Rd in Fulbaria. From here the rickshaw fare to nearby hotels is usually Tk 2-3, to further away places like the YMCA on New Eskaton Rd costs Tk 4-5.

If you arrive by boat from Khulna or Barisal, launches dock at Saddarghat while the BIWTC 'Rocket' ferries dock at Badam Tole. The rickshaw fare to nearby hotels is Tk 2-3, further afield to places like the YMCA costs Tk 6. Do not take rickshaws on Buckland Bund as they tend to be expensive, if you walk out of the Bund to Islampur Rd there are many rickshaws there.

Local Transport Urban transport in Dacca consists mainly of rickshaws although minibuses and buses are on the increase. Taxis and babytaxis are few, and these tend to be found outside the Hotel Sonargaon. Within the city perimeter taxi fares are usually no more than Tk 40, babytaxis are Tk 15. Of course there are no meters. Scooter microbuses occasionally appear on the streets and can carry six passengers. Fares are Tk 1-1.50 but they're rare.

If you intend to make any lengthy trips across or through town and don't want to take a taxi you can take a bus or minibus; use rickshaws for short distances only. When using rickshaws to get to hotels, be sure to give the street name, not the name of the establishment. Most drivers don't know hotel names and are likely to take you on a tour of the city in search of your destination – all with a higher fare in mind. Rickshaw fares should be about Tk 1 per km, within the city perimeter fares are usually Tk 3-4.

Buses are by far the cheapest method of transport, the only problem is that they have no signs in English and their numbering is likewise only in Bangala. Furthermore they are always overcrowded so boarding between major bus stops is virtually impossible. Bus fares vary from Tk 0.30 to 2.50. There are now a handful of double decker buses operating in Dacca.

A few routes that may be of use are:

No 6 ৬ – to International Airport and Central Railway Station at Kamalapur.
No 9 ৯ – Farm Gate to Mirpur and back again.
Nos 2 ২ & 20 ২০ Farm Gate to Mirpur (use one of these to get to the zoo).
No 5 ৫ – Banani to Fulbaria via the Mogh Bazar and Farm Gate.

Bus No 6 usually goes right to the Central Railway Station via Farm Gate, Mogh Bazar, Gulistan (Fulbaria), Motijheel. These are the major bus stops, key points in the city area where rickshaws are available for short distances. Buses to the suburbs of Savar, Pagla, Narayanganj, Sonargaon and other outlying towns and villages can usually be found around Fulbaria.

AROUND DACCA

Savar

Savar, 36 km north-east of Dacca, is located on the banks of the Dhakeswari River. It is an important commercial centre boasting a model farm village. The Jahangir Nagar University is also located here. Savar is being developed into an industrial centre, particularly for pharmaceutical products. The Bangladesh Rice Research Institute is here also.

On the Dacca-Aricha road in Savar the 50-metre high Jatiyo Shaheed Smriti Sangha is shaped like a delta-winged spacecraft and was built to commemorate those who died in the fight for freedom.

Other places of interest are the palace of the Rajah of Bhawal, and two km out in the village of Majidpur are traces of a fort and a palace or temple from the Pala period. Market day in Savar is Tuesday when it gets very busy on the banks of the Savar River. There is a group of Badhi river-gypsy people here. Their snake charmers have their village a little to the north of town.

Dhamrai

Dhamrai is on the banks of the Bangshi River, 32 km north-west of Dacca and near Savar. This is a particularly ancient site, dating back to the Pala dynasty, containing Hindu temples and possibly an early Buddhist settlement. The town now has handloom factories producing saris.

Pajendrapur National Park

This forest park with its varied birdlife is 53 km north of Dacca. It's noted for angling and boating on the long meandering lake. There are six resthouses scattered through the 65,000 hectare park.

Sonargaon

The 'City of Panam' was one of the ancient capitals of Bangala, the seat of the 13th-century Chandra and Deva dynasties. During the Sultanate period the city became known as the Seat of the Mighty Majesty and was a highly developed metropolis. The sultanate collapsed under pressure from the Moghul expansion in 1611, but they considered its location too exposed to Portuguese and Mogh pirates and established Dacca as their capital.

At its height Sonargaon was an impressive place. Mu Huang, the 15th century Chinese traveller, commented on the surrounding moat, broad streets, great mausoleums and other cosmopolitan features. Earlier, in the 14th century, Ibn Battuta had also paid a visit but under the Moghuls it deteriorated and the decline had gone so far that under the British it simply faded away.

When you arrive in Sonargaon from Dacca rickshaws cluster on the roadside near the bus stop. To the right of the roadway is a bricked road to Mograpara. It is a bit over a km and about Tk 3 by rickshaw to the mausoleum of Ghiazzuddin Azam Shah (1399-1440). The mazhar area is walled with a small archway into a courtyard. To the right is a row of tombs and to the left is the mausoleum. The twin structures are of traditional Bangala-Muslim architecture with the peculiar Bangala roof style. Pilgrims still visit this place, they carry candles and have come to ask a favour.

Getting There Sonargaon is 28 km east of Dacca, a half-hour Tk 5 ride on the bus to the Meghna River. After you cross the river ask for Sonargaon to ensure you get off at the right place.

Goaldi

Eight km north of Sonargaon this village is known as the City of Panam. Tourist brochures refer to the mosque here but make little mention of the fine traditional houses known as *havelis*. The mosque dates from 1519 and is a perfect specimen of Saracenic architecture. There is another mosque dating from 1522 in Saidpur and a six-domed mosque from the same period in Mogampur – both little known.

The route from Sonargaon is partly paved, partly brick, partly dirt. On the way you pass a curious baroque structure with statues fronting a large pond. This ramshackle building has recently been turned into a local museum. The village of Goaldi is a pleasant surprise with it's ornate colonnaded and pedimented structures tightly packed around the narrow lanes.

Narayanganj

This town, 24 km to the east of Dacca beyond Pagla, was once the business centre for Sonargaon and still maintains some sense of its former trading days though the port is gradually silting up. Some dredging is being carried out, but very slowly and with very primitive equipment. Nowadays textiles are the main source of industry and the new buildings that house them often hide the remnants of architecture from more illustrious days. Narayanganj remains the largest centre of the jute industry, while the handloom industry at Baburhat is known locally as the Manchester of the East.

Interesting historical sites such as old forts are located along the Sitalakhaya. The hexagonal Hadjiganj Fort is on the west bank in the area of Khizpur. Like the Idrakpur Fort it has a large circular structure. A km and a half further down is the rectangular Sonakanda fort on the east bank. At the village of Nabiganj is the beautiful 18th century Qadam Rasul Gateway.

Getting There A bus from Fulbaria in Dacca costs Tk 3 to Narayanganj. An early start from Dacca through Pagla and Narayanganj would give you enough time to cover Munshinganj and Vikrampur. The usual route back is via Narayanganj, as the launches and ferries to Dacca seldom stop in Munshinganj. Via Narayanganj you can stop for dinner at the Mary Anderson Floating Restaurant at Pagla on your way back to the city. Pagla also has a Hindu temple and a medieval Moghul bridge, now in ruins.

Munshinganj

This subdivision of the district of Dacca is bounded in the east and south by the Dhakeswari, the Meghna and the Padma. The small town is actually quite a busy port; it's like a tiny version of Narayanganj with old and new buildings, quaint little arched bridges over small nalas and old temples fronted with ponds.

The Idrakpur Fort in Munshinganj is half sunk in the ground but wholly intact. The curious 10-metre-high circular platform may once have been a gun emplacement. Photography is restricted here as the compound houses the jail and the quarters for the Senior Subdivisional Officer. Ask the SDO for permission. The Ichamata River has completely dried up here, there is nothing left except for a small trickle.

Getting There It costs Tk 2.50 for the 2½ hour launch trip from Narayanganj to Munshinganj. It only costs Tk 2 and only takes two hours from Dacca but the trip from Narayanganj is more scenic and picturesque than on the Buriganga. From the launch ghat it costs Tk 2 by rickshaw to the Idrakpur Fort.

Vikrampur

This town is 12 km west of Munshinganj near Hasmat Budjsaguganj. It was once the domain of Rajah Chandragupta, king of Ujjain in India. It later became the seat of administration for a Brahmin-Buddhist king named Rampal, the son of Manipala who ruled this part of Bangala from 1084 to 1130. It was to here that Lakshamanasena fled when his kingdom in Kahnauti fell to the Khiljis Muslims. The rajbari – area of the king – here is called Rampal. It's just a little village with traces of ancient Buddhist and Hindu palaces and temples.

There is also a mazhar and the old six-domed pre-Moghul (1483) mosque of Baba Adam, complete with the usual architectural features of the period. A rickshaw will take you there via a rough dirt road for Tk 40.

Getting There See the Narayanganj information for travel details.

MYMENSINGH DISTRICT

The district of Mymensingh, located immediately north of the districts of Tangail and Dacca, is the largest in Bangladesh. It borders the Indian state of Meghalaya to the north, spans the Jamuna in the west and the Meghna in the east. The northern boundary is limited by the low, wooded chain of hills called the Meghalaya. In the foothills and lowlands swampy regions abound, making the region almost impenetrable. Rice paddies and jute plantations are common in the wet flatlands.

The early history of the region is still indistinct, no archaeological finds of any note have been made here, restricting any speculation as to who or what occupied the region. Only with the arrival of the Tuglukhs in the 13th century does the history become definite. The mosques are only pre-Moghul and Moghul in style. The five-domed Qutb Mosque, ornately embellished with terracotta artwork characteristic of the period, is the most notable. In the village of Egarasindur are two notable Moghul mosques – the Sadi Mosque of 1652 and the Shah Mohammed Mosque of 1680.

While neglected by its Moghul overlords, the region received its greatest moment of glory when the British ruled during the time of jute's zenith on the international commodity market. The whole region became one vast jute plantation; it grew better and of a higher quality here than anywhere else. It still remains one of Bangladesh's principal export crops.

The borders of this district were drawn arbitrarily under the Radcliffe Boundary Award, announced during Partition. As a consequence, it divided many of the original tribes of the area, leaving some in India, others in Bangladesh. These tribes seem to bear some linguistic connection with the people of Nepal. They include Hindus and Buddhists although most of them are animists.

MYMENSINGH

The outskirts of Mymensingh give a slightly deceptive appearance to its nature;

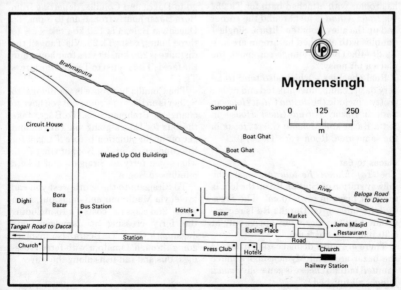

many modern buildings which house various colleges and the Kumudini Hospital greet the new arrival. However, the further one goes into the town the more the original impression diminishes: the scene reverts back to the usual chaos of Bangladeshi urban life.

There are the usual left-overs from the British planters and their administration, but overall the strongest impression is of a place wholly untouched or for that matter untroubled by the events of the world beyond its boundaries. The central section of the city, the *saddar*, is hidden by trees and walls from the main roadway. A minaret towers over it all. The railway station is here, just near a small church. Numerous post-independence mixed with the old contribute to the hotch-potch nature of the town centre.

The Brahmaputra River separates the town from the jute plantations and mills in the village of Samoganj, 2½ km away.

Places to Stay

Hotel Uttara on Station Rd is newish and has rooms with attached bath for Tk 25/40. *Hotel Ashad* is just around the corner and up the alley from the Uttara. Singles/doubles with attached bathroom are also Tk 25/40. The TV lounge can make the place a bit noisy.

Real cheapies – which also tend to be very basic, damp, unventilated and rather grotty – include the *Jostna Guest House* in Sadesh Bazar, *Nirala Guest House* in Satta Bazar and *Momota Guest House* in the same area. Rooms are Tk 20/40.

Places to Eat

The *Taj Mahal Restaurant*, near the railway station on Station Rd on the left, is the best place in town to eat. The *Press Club Restaurant* on Durgha Rd is recommended by the locals but opens only at 6.30 pm, closes at 9 pm.

There are some dismal eating places in the bazar area and Mymensingh's much vaunted buffalo cheese is generally *paowa jaina* – all finished.

Getting There & Away

The district is to a great degree isolated, and access is only by road from Dacca and rail from Rangpur. The Jamuna River excludes any easy traffic with the adjacent divisions of Rajshahi, and the Meghna likewise cuts off Chittagong.

There are two ways from Dacca; one via Tangail, the other via Baloga which is the quickest.

Rail Train services, daily frequencies and fares from Mymensingh include:

to	freq	1st	2nd	3rd
Dacca	4 daily	Tk 83	TK 21	TK 9
Comilla	2 daily	Tk 155	TK 38	TK 16.50
Rangpur	4 daily	Tk 179	Tk 47	Tk 21
Dinajpur	2 daily	Tk 203	Tk 52	Tk 25
Bogra	2 daily	Tk 160	Tk 39	Tk 18

To Sylhet via Comilla get off at Akhaura Junction for the connection.

Road The BRTC and private buses only go to Dacca and Comilla, departing from Bora Bazar hourly from 6 am to 3 pm. To Dacca via Baloga is 120 km, takes 2½ to three hours, costs Tk 23. Via Tangail the distance is 200 km, it takes four hours and the fare is Tk 31. Just to Tangail the fare is Tk 15.

The Comilla bus route is via Baloga; to Sylhet is on the same route but you have to change at Brahmanbaria. To Bogra take the bus for Dacca going via Tangail and get off at the junction before Tangail for the connecting bus for Boapur Ghat from where you ferry to Sirajganj and take a minibus to Bogra.

To Sirajganj to the south-west you can travel via Madhupur and Jamalpur, from where 2nd class rail costs Tk 15 including the ferry crossing at Jamalganj and Jagannath Ghat. To Bogra also involves going through Jamalpur with ferry crossings, bus and rail trips along the way.

DACCA-MYMENSINGH

If you take the Tangail route between Dacca and Mymensingh, in the village of Egarasindur on the old Brahmaputra River there are two lovely old mosques. The Saadi Mosque of 1652 is a unique building with a single large dome towering over two smaller ones. Four corners have short towers and the main entrance is framed with carved and painted patterns. The Shah Mohammed Mosque of 1680 has a single dome and is fronted by another structure which serves as a gateway, called a *dachala*

Hatiya Jama Mosque, Tangail

Khulna Division

Of all the divisions of Bangladesh, Khulna is marked most by the fingers of the Ganges, those tributaries which sluice down into the Bay of Bengal, creating a vast maze of waterways. Almost all the division is drained by innumerable streams and creeks, making two-thirds of Khulna marshland or dense jungle and an absolute haven for wildlife. The southern part of Khulna, called the *Sundarbans* (beautiful forest), is the best example of this lush delta vegetation.

Khulna is in the south-west of Bangladesh and borders with the state of West Bengal in India. In the north the Ganga slices it off from the Rajshahi division while to the east the Padma, a river formed by the confluent streams of the Ganga and the Jamuna, divide it from the Dacca division.

Because its topography is unstable and difficult to traverse Khulna has no great history of early settlement although Ptolemy mentioned the existence of two cities in this region. Xuan Zhang came to the country in the 7th century AD but failed to note the jungles in this region. The first recorded period of habitation was in the 13th century when Hindus from

the north fled here to escape the onslaught of the invading Moghuls. They sought refuge right in the middle of the jungle of the Sundarbans, where they constructed their temples, palaces and ghats. The pressure of the Moghuls also sent both Khiljis and Afghan Muslims to the region where they also established their kingdoms and built mosques and palaces.

The dense jungles and numerous rivers formed natural barriers to any invasion from the west or east. Even after its late settlement it remained relatively neglected by the Moghuls and it was not until the arrival of the British that it started to be developed. Nowadays, some of the largest jute mills, match factories, cold storage for fish and shrimps, cable factories, some of the largest jute mills, and the only newsprint mill in the country have been set up here. Except for matches all these manufactured products are shipped out through the port of Mongla. The division also has a large power station and a variety of transportation links to Dacca, Rajshahi and to India. Khulna ranks behind Chittagong as the third most industrialized area in the country.

There are six districts in the Khulna

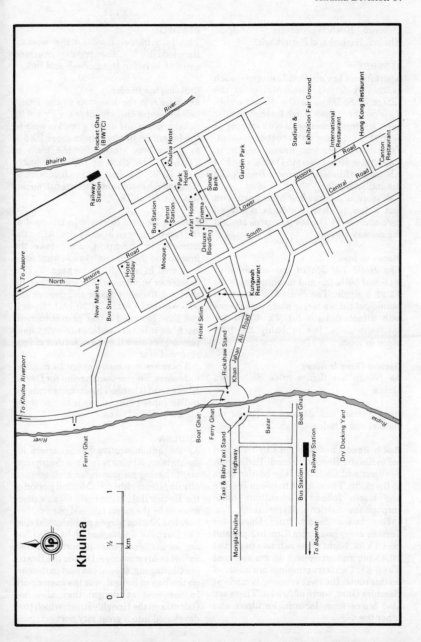

division: Kushtia, Jessore, Faridpur, Khulna, Barisal and Patuakhali.

JESSORE

Apart from a few medieval mosques, such as the six-domed Jama Masjid in the village of Sailkupa in the Jhenida sub-division, there is not much for the traveller here. Its importance rests with its role as central road-junction for the division. From here you can travel north to Rajshahi or Bogra, east to Dacca, south to Khulna and Mongla, or west to Benopol on the Indian border.

Jessore is a sprawling little town with just a few modern buildings scattered here and there. The town centres around the railway station.

Places to Stay

The *Hotel Taj Mahal* has rooms with attached bath, fan and mosquito nets for Tk 20 a single. The *Hotel Mid-Town*, on Municipal Rd is a larger place with rooms with attached bath for Tk 45/60 for singles/doubles. It's probably the best place in town.

Getting There & Away

Air Biman has flights twice daily from Dacca.

River Ferries link Jessore to Dacca via Barisal and Khulna.

Rail & Road There are links by road and rail to Khulna, Benopol, Ishurdi, Parbatipur, Syedpur and Chiliharti, the border town to the north. The rail link between Jessore and Dacca follows a circuitous route through the district of Mymensingh.

Day buses depart from Dacca for Jessore every hour from 6 am to 3 pm and cost Tk 55. Night express buses depart at 10.45 pm and arrive at 7.45 am and cost Tk 60-65. Two ferry crossings are involved on this route, the river crossing is made at Bandura Ghat, south of Aricha. There are also buses from Ishurdi, Faridpur and other towns.

BENOPOL

This is a border town on the west of Bangladesh, it's the regular overland gateway between Bangladesh and India.

Crossing the Border

Exiting From the bus-stop to the Bangladesh border checkpoint costs Tk 4-6 by rickshaw. It is just under a one km walk to the Indian border, and from there Rs 5-6 to the railway station for the train to Calcutta. The 2½ hour trip to Calcutta costs Rs 6. The limit for reconversion of Bangladesh money into foreign currencies was last set at Tk 500.

Entering Be sure to arrive in Benopol at the latest between 3 and 4 pm. After the immigration checkpost, don't take the first bus on the right unless you want to be crammed in with all the luggage. Take a coaster or minibus which are further up the road; these are faster and cleaner and well worth the extra Tk 20 cost. Even if you have reserved a seat grab it immediately as it is very difficult to evict local passengers once they have settled in your reserved seat.

There are minibuses every 20 minutes to Jessore, a major transit point for Dacca, Khulna and Ishurdi. The exchange rate for Indian rupees into takkas is better at the border than in Dacca.

KHULNA

As the administrative headquarters for the division, Khulna is rather a disappointment, having no particular architectural offerings from either the Moghul period or the British Raj. In general, it was a place ignored by the major colonial powers. Not only has Khulna played no historical role, like Dacca or Chittagong, it has also had no earlier economic importance, like Sylhet or Mymensingh. During the British era Chittagong, the old sea port in the east on the Bay of Bengal, was the major port. In the west of Bengal they also had Calcutta on the Hooghly River, which they developed into a great city port

It is only recently that a measure of industrial and commercial development has come to the city. Chittagong port, unable to handle all of the trade that has come its way, has given Khulna's river ports on the Rupsa and at Mongla a considerable amount of business. This in turn has brought a number of industries to Khulna, attracted by the availability of transport.

On arrival in the city you are likely to be misled by the size and nature of the place; it seems very small and old. This is the old section of the city, neglected since liberation. The old part of the city is mainly bazars and narrow lanes dating from the Raj era. Prior to the arrival of the British there were just small settlements on the banks of the Rupsa to the south and the Bhairab to the north.

After independence Khulna expanded to the south-east but even here the streets are narrow. It is in the Upper Jessore Rd area that the most developed section of the city is to be found. This is where the best hotels and the New Market are. The cinemas, Chinese restaurants and government offices are on the Lower Jessore Rd.

Despite the development of Khulna as a port the Rupsa River here is not deep enough to handle ocean-going vessels. Mongla, previously known as the port of Chalna, has been developed as the modern port for Khulna and the new Mongla Highway is under construction across the Rupsa River.

There is not much to see in Khulna apart from the medieval nine-domed Jama Masjid in Majidpur village. Khulna is mainly a jumping off point to Bagerhat and Mongla or the Sundarbans, or a transit point to Benopol.

Information

There is officially no tourist info centre in Khulna but the Khulna Municipal Board in the Hotel Selim will provide information when required. Foreign currency can be exchanged at the Sonali Bank. Handicrafts can be found at the New Market on North Jessore Rd.

Places to Stay – bottom end

In the centre of town on Jessore Rd *Deluxe Boarding* has clean rooms with shared bath for Tk 15/25 for singles/doubles. It's good value and within walking distance of the BIWTC ghat and the bus stations. *Hotel Light*, 1 Boroda Dutta Lane near the power house, is also good value with singles/doubles at Tk 25/40.

In the Khulna Bazar area the *Hotel Khulna* has shared bath rooms at Tk 25/30. After you pay for your room wait for a receipt or they'll try to charge you twice. And take care not to allow anyone into your room. Behind the Sonali Bank the *Arafat Hotel International* has fairly clean rooms with attached bath for Tk 30/50 for singles/doubles.

Places to Stay – middle

Hotel Park is right in the centre on Khulna Bazar Rd and is modern and clean with rooms with attached bath at Tk 50/75. There is a restaurant on the ground floor. This is the closest hotel to the 'Rocket' dock.

Hotel Selim (tel 20191) on Shamsur Rahman Rd is another old and established place. There's a restaurant, bar and TV lounge and rooms with attached bath are Tk 55-65 for singles, Tk 75-95 for doubles, Tk 200 for an aircon suite. The Khulna Municipal Board has recently taken over management of the hotel from the Parjatan Tourism Corporation.

Places to Stay – top end

Hotel Rupsa International (tel 61563) on North Jessore Rd has double rooms at Tk 100 or with aircon at Tk 175. Also on North Jessore Rd the *Hotel Holiday* will apparently have a bar and swimming pool and will probably replace the Rupsa as Khulna's best hotel when completed.

Places to Eat

The *King Hua Chinese Restaurant* on

Shamsur Rd opposite the Hotel Selim has tolerably good cuisine with prices similar to any of Bangladesh's many locally run Chinese restaurants. Like other similar restaurants it is open from 11 am to 3 pm and from 6 to 10.30 pm.

The *Canton Restaurant* on South Central Rd is locally popular and also has fair food. Note that they have no coffee and their 'jasmine tea' is just local brown tea. On Lower Jessore Rd the *Hongkong Restaurant* also has the same standard Chinese cuisine and a local chef. It does have coffee but otherwise it's nothing special. The *International Chinese Restaurant* is also on Lower Jessore Rd, a few blocks north of the Hongkong. It opens only in the evenings.

The *Hotel Selim Restaurant* is quite pricey with breakfast costing Tk 24. They have a bar here with beer by the can at Tk 30. The *Hotel Park Restaurant* does a good semi-western breakfast for just Tk 10. Meals here cost Tk 12-16 and are good value.

Getting There & Away

Air Biman has two flights a day from Dacca via Jessore for Tk 300. There are flights via Jessore to Chittagong once weekly. The Bangladesh Biman office (tel 61020-63) is on North Jessore Rd.

River There is one 'Rocket' ferry daily from Dacca. The 24-hour trip costs Tk 424 in 1st class, Tk 257 in 2nd, Tk 124 in Interclass, Tk 70 in 3rd. See the map for the location of the BIWTC 'Rocket' ghat.

From Chittagong you can travel to Khulna by river via Barisal but you might have to wait a few hours or even overnight to make the connection. The 36-hour trip costs Tk 284 plus 212 in 1st class for the two sectors, Tk 189 plus 126 in 2nd, Tk 85 plus 62 in Interclass, Tk 57 plus 35 in 3rd.

There are also BIWTC 'Rocket' ferries to Mongla. The trip takes about two hours and costs Tk 15 in 3rd class. If you're going to Mongla it's preferable to go by road.

Rail From Dacca the train takes a long and roundabout route. Fares for the 24-hour trip are Tk 275 in 1st class or Tk 495 in 1st class aircon. There are also trains to Khulna from Chiliharti, Bogra and Ishurdi. The railway station is near the BIWTC ghat.

Road There are buses to Khulna from Dacca via Jessore; Benopol via Jessore; Bogra and Rajshahi via Ishurdi. A new highway is being constructed from Dacca which will cross the Jamuna River south of the current crossing at Bandura Ghat which serves both Jessore and Khulna. This will cut travel time to Khulna from Dacca. At present the trip takes about 12 hours and the fare is Tk 60.

From Ishurdi the bus to Khulna is preferable if you depart in the morning but by night the train is better. The Midnight Express departs for Khulna at 12.30 am. You may have to wait for it but there is a lounge for 1st class travellers where they check tickets. For food the railway restaurant is poor value, eating places outside near the bus terminal are better – they serve fresh steaming rice, hot chappatis and good curry. It's wise to book 1st class tickets well ahead but 2nd and 3rd class are booked just half an hour before departure. It's also possible to get off at Jessore and take a minibus from there to Khulna. The rail fares are Tk 125 in 1st class, Tk 31.50 in 2nd, Tk 13.50 in 3rd. The minibus between Jessore and Khulna takes 1½ hours and costs Tk 2.50.

Take a babytaxi Tk 20, minibus Tk 15 or taxi Tk 25 to get from Khulna to Mongla.

Getting Around

It's advisable to allow plenty of time to catch a bus or train when departing Khulna. It's quite a distance to the boat ghat on the Rupsa River though it's not necessary to go all the way up to the ferry ghat, unless you have your own vehicle to transport across. The boat ghat is right at the end of Khan Jahan Ali Rd. It is only Tk 3 to the ghat, a boat across is Tk 0.25 and entrance fee to the ghat is Tk 0.15.

Take a boat that goes right to the other boat ghat. There is a lane here through a bazar which leads to the railway and the minibus stations. It's a short walk from here but from the ferry ghat where the Mongla Highway begins there are two lanes to the railway station, about a quarter of a km away. The lower lane goes via the bazar, the upper lane by the highway is longer – a minibus usually waits for passengers from the railway station.

BAGERHAT

This quiet little town is 40 km south-east of Khulna on the northern fringes of the Sundarbans. The Muslim mystic Khan Jahan Ali is reputed to have settled down here in the middle of the 15th century, after decades of wandering. A mausoleum was raised to his memory and no less than 360 mosques in the region are dedicated to his memory. Like Sheikh Jallalud-din of Sylhet and Qalandar Shah Baz of Sehwan Sharif in Sind in Pakistan this sufi mystic became well known as a holy man.

Like most of the sufis that settled in the subcontinent in medieval times he must have come from West Asia, where sufism originated. Sufis are Muslim mystics, the counterparts of the sadhus or yogis of India. They are concerned with mysticism in life and use means such as yoga and meditation to attain union with the omnipotent eternal being.

The town's two principal attractions are a few km outside at the village of Sat Gombad.

Sat Gombad Mosque

Built in 1459 the Sat Gombad Mosque is located in a village named after it. There is not even a tiny railway station here. The trains simply stops at a place marked by a few tea shops and a cluster of rickshaws.

You may wish to have a cup of tea and savour the tranquil air before taking a rickshaw to the mosque.

The village roads are narrow but paved and run through wooded areas occasionally opening out to rice paddies and villages of thatched huts. The Sat Gombad Mosque is a little to the north of the village and is more impressive for its rustic location than for any feat of construction. It's fairly large, rectangular like a church and in an open clearing with a lawn around it, fronted by a brick archway. Behind it is a large *dighi* with lotus flowers surrounded on all sides with coconut trees except on the mosque side.

The mosque is all brickwork with 77 little domes and four short towers at the corners. On top, right in the middle, is the usual curvilinear Bangala thatch roof placed there as an insignia or a symbol of Bangala architecture. Or simply as decoration! It is not really functional like a bell tower. The whole structure is massive, with a dark veneer of age, and inscrutably impressive in the quiet rustic atmosphere. Close to it is a primary school, usually with the children out playing in the field. Along the pond into the nearby villages is a pleasant walk.

Mazhar Khan Jahan Ali

To get to this shrine you have to backtrack on the same road until you come to another paved road, heading west. This road leads through woods and occasional grainfields right to the entrance to the mazhar. The squat quadrangular brick structure has a single dome and is of the same traditional design as the nearby mosque.

The cenotaph, seen right at the entrance, is apparently covered with tiles of various colours and inscribed with Koranic verses but is usually covered with a red cloth embroidered with gold threads. The shrine and the nearby mosque are enclosed by a massive wall with short towers at each corner and archways on the roadside and on the rear, where a pond is located. There is a tiny bazar with teashops which caters to pilgrims who come to buy rosewater in bottles and joss sticks as offerings at the cenotaph.

As you enter the premises the fakirs will stir on sighting you and commence calling on Allah. They're close relations of the spiritual mendicants, both Hindu and Muslim, you find all over the subcontinent. The main entrance to the shrine faces an archway where stone steps lead down to a fairly large pond. It is here where the faithful wash their heads, ears, hands and arms (up to the elbows at least), and feet before solemnly putting on their white skullcap and veil. They light incense sticks before bowing down in silent prayer.

Among the faithful are Hindu womenfolk and children, dressed in clothes which have become grey and grimy from age. The women usually come to collect their water supply in earthen pots which, full or empty, they carry on their left hip, held by the crook of the left arm. The children, mostly girls with matted long hair,

usually have a dip in the pond and try to catch fish with their little clay pots, presumably baited by bits of food clinging to its inner side.

Settings like this are always peaceful, quiet and serene. I sat on the ghat steps, overhung with tree branches, and a little girl wandered up, clutching her earthen pot, and whispered something to me, almost like a lonely sadhu in a secluded hut on the edge of the lake in Pushkar I once saw talking to someone beloved but unseen on the water. She walked away then came back, seemingly asking questions in a soft manner, like on a stage. There was no communication as it was all in Bangala. She was interrupted by another little girl in cleaner clothes but unhappy looking – perhaps about the errand she was sent on – to beg.

Meanwhile the women on a step lower down talked some more to me, and since there was no reply she stood up and sat on the elevated side of the steps and produced out of her pot a little fish. Successful, she smiled. She then began talking, more to herself or the little fish than to me. She wasn't begging, quite a lady despite her grubby clothes, her little pot and fish. She won me over and a takka fled from me to her.

Mazhar of Khan Jahan Ali

Places to Stay

The *Parjatan Inn* has cooking facilities and rooms from Tk 20 to 50. There are four other hotels, all close together and with rates from Tk 15 to 25.

Getting There & Away

There are six trains daily to Bagerhat from Khulna, the earliest departing at 7.30 am. The trip takes about 2½ hours to Sat Gombad, the village before Bagerhat, and costs Tk 3. By getting off here you avoid having to backtrack from Bagerhat to the two principal points of interest at this village. There are also minibuses but they tend to wait a long time, the train is preferable. It's not crowded, more comfortable and there's more opportunity to socialise with the local passengers, some of them pilgrims on their way to the shrine. It's a pleasant ride through a luxuriant and peaceful rural landscape. The trains stops at three tiny villages. By contrast the minibuses are crowded and cramped and passengers are prone to suddenly throwing up. Furthermore the drivers tend to be reckless and always in a hurry. Take the train!

From Sat Gombad you can take a rickshaw to visit the mosque and shrine. Rural rickshaws are honest but it is still wise to fix the rate; usually the round trip from the Sat Gombad train halt to the mosque and the shrine and then to Bagerhat will be about Tk 15 including some waiting time. If you want more time at each spot you can travel the 5½ km from the teashops to the mosque for Tk 3-4, from the mosque to the shrine will be Tk 3-4 again and from the shrine to Bagerhat, six km distance, will be Tk 5.

Minibuses on their way to Khulna from Bagerhat pass through Sat Gombad, but they are usually packed to capacity so it is preferable to go to Bagerhat and start from there. There are a few tea stalls and fruit vendors near the bus station. If you're in a hurry to get back to Khulna then minibuses depart almost every 15 minutes and the fare is Tk 8. Or you can take your time and wait for the train which departs about every 1½ hours. On the train you have to put up with beggars but they are generally not insistent, on the minibuses they can only look up to you from outside.

Apparently there are launches from Bagerhat to Khulna but they are infrequent and the trip is long, though supposedly pleasant, and costs Tk 30. Another route involves a stream crossing just out of Bagerhat, then a rickshaw to the bus station and a bus to Pirojpur, another 'Rocket' stopping point, from where you can get a launch to Barisal.

MONGLA

This is the main port of Khulna. It lies 38 km to the south and was established after the silting up of Chalna. It is the international port for trade from this division, but is also known as the gateway to the Sundarbans.

As the administrative centre of the subdivision Mongla has a few government offices and billets, shops, a boarding house, one hotel and one cinema. Nothing is beyond walking distance, though there are a few hopeful rickshaws. Perhaps these work in tandem with the brothel-village called Bari Shantari where you can slake your thirst in more senses than one as they serve liquor as well.

River life here has an international air with the local watercraft dwarfed by gigantic ocean-going vessels. The whole riverfront is made up of ghats belonging to the Port Authority, the navy, the BIWTC, the public ghats and others. Here you can see black rowboats, fast patrol boats, Port Authority launches and tug boats, passenger launches, large country cargo boats and sail boats. Here you may see the little black boats with their curved prows and bows, usually rowed with two crossed paddles by a single boatman. You may also see them up in the Chittagong Hill Tracts on Kaptai Lake

Boat movement in the channel is almost ceaseless with launches coming or going, tug boats with barges in tow, black boats ferrying passengers across the river, larger ones going to outlying villages, patrol boats departing for the

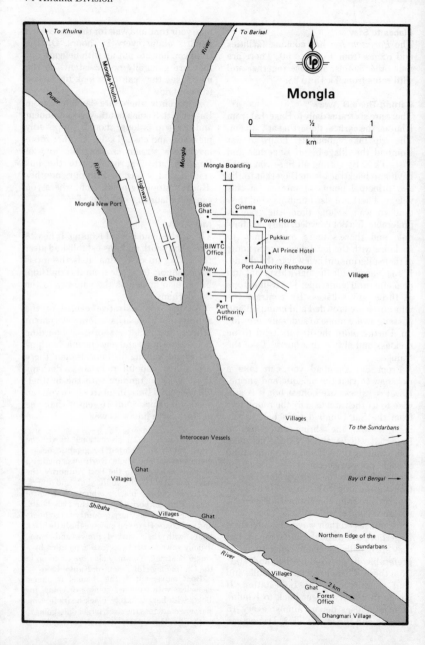

Sundarbans or the ocean-going vessels lying at anchor at the confluence of the Pusur and the Mongla Nala. Women and children in small craft cluster round the large ships, doing barter trade with the sailors. Speedboats skim past native sailboats or oar boats laden with wood from the Sundarbans.

Places to Stay & Eat

Stay at the *Port Authority Resthouse* (tel 303) which has a restaurant; rooms are Tk 90/125 with bath. Apply first to the Estate Officer, no prior permission is required from Khulna.

The *Al-Prince Hotel* (tel 454) is fairly old but seems to be where the action is: there is a dining hall which serves as both the local bar and dance hall. It seems to be open till midnight. The rooms, most of which require at least some repair work, are Tk 25 for a single and Tk 45 for a double. You can get breakfast here for Tk 9, curry dishes and salad for Tk 18-25, and a variety of foreign canned beer at Tk 30.

At the bottom end is the run down old *Mongla Boarding* which has rooms with and without attached bath from Tk 17/30 for singles/doubles.

Getting There

Khulna-Mongla Though only 38 km from Khulna it is still advisable to make an early start. The river trip takes about two hours, ferries cost Tk 15, launches Tk 12. By road you first have to take a rickshaw down to the boat ghat and from the other side of the Rupsa River babytaxis, minibuses and taxis wait for passengers at the start of the Mongla Highway. Fares are Tk 20 by babytaxi, Tk 15 by minibus, Tk 25 by taxi.

The highway is very new and wide and for a third of the way it is well paved but it is likely to be some time before the rest is completed. The uncompleted road is dirt or gravel. The route runs through open country passing the village of Degras on the right, where a fish processing factory has been set up.

Before departing from Khulna, check

with the Divisional Forest Officer for any appropriate permit if you want to visit the Sundarbans. They also have information on the plantlife and wildlife of the region and on transportation possibilities and possible tours. This is also a good place to attempt to hitch a free/cheap lift on one of the Port Authority boats down to Heron Point (Nilkamal), right on the coastal strip of the Sundarbans. The Port Authority can also sometimes arrange for you to go on an ocean-going vessel with the pilot. The pilots are let off or collected at Heron Point.

Other River Transport There are BIWTC 'Rocket' ferries to Barisal and Dacca. Barisal takes 12 hours with fares of Tk 164 in 1st class, Tk 99 in 2nd, Tk 45 in Interclass and Tk 30 in 3rd. Dacca is 24 hours away and fares are Tk 366 in 1st, Tk 222 in 2nd, Tk 100 in Interclass and Tk 67 in 3rd. Only 1st and 2nd class require pre-booking. It's a five-hour launch trip to Bagerhat and costs Tk 13.

Mongla-Heron Point For boats from Mongla down to Heron Point check with the Port Authority officials. They usually have launches taking pilots down at three to four-day intervals although pilots are only taken down when a foreign vessel has arrived and requires guiding up through the narrow Pusur channel.

Alternatively you can try the Forest Officer in the village of Dhangmari. The office is on the northern edge of the Sundarbans, four km by boat via the confluence of the Pusur and the Mongla Nala, in an inlet where the land begins to be really forested. The trip to Dhangmari takes about an hour each way and hourly boat hire is Tk 30-40 plus baksheesh. Alternatively take a passenger boat to a village on what appears to be a peninsula in the river. Villages here have individual bamboo jetties jutting out to the confluence. Local boats ply between these villages and Mongla for Tk 1.50 but it is still about a two km walk down a muddy

The Rocket Ferry

track to Dhangmari. If the Forest Officer is not there his staff may still be able to arrange a boat if you have a fairly large party. If you succeed in getting to Heron Point you can stay at the *Port Authority Staff House*.

Getting Around

Minibuses, taxis and other transport cluster a little past the new river port of Mongla. Just beyond is the footpath which leads to a brick track to a ghat from where boats ferry passengers across to the town proper. The ghat entrance fee is Tk 0.25 and the ferry fare is Tk 0.75. The walk over the bund and brick track is about 10 minutes.

SUNDARBANS NATIONAL PARK

The Sundarbans, making up the southern half of the Khulna Division, are the largest littoral mangrove belt in the world, stretching 80 km into the hinterland from the coast. The Sundarbans cover an area of 38,500 square km, of which about one third is covered in water. Six ranges make up the region – at partition Bashirat and Namkhona went to India while Chandpai, Sharankhola, Hulna and Satkhira went to Bangladesh. The Sundarbans are bound by the Bhaleswari River in the east, the Bay of Bengal to the south, the Khulna district to the north and the Raimangal and Haringhata Rivers to the west. The tiny island of Talpatty emerges at the western boundary in the Bay of Bengal. At one time the mangrove forests extended even further but during the Afghan, Moghul and British periods the forests in Barisal, Patuakhali and Noakhali were hewn down for agricultural purposes.

The impenetrable forests of the Sundarbans begin near the village of Dhangmari, where the Bhairab and Pusur Rivers meet. For about 60 km to the south there are no settlements of any kind. There are no permanent settlements within the forest apart from a few government workforce camps housing the labour force for the extraction of timber. These camps are all either built on stilts or they 'hang' from the trees because of the soft ground and the two-metre tides that course through the coastal areas. The ground is all bog, down to a depth of about three metres. The workforce numbers about 20,000 although that number more than doubles during the months of April and May.

The climate of the region is considered moderate: annual rainfall of 1850 mm (73 inches), a mild winter and humid summer (88% humidity). The ecological balance, as with all tidal environments, is extremely delicate, and is influenced greatly by tidal shifts which affect the salinity, and hence the growth rates in the surrounding vegetation. A vast amount of sediment is carried down from India via the Ganges and dumped in the Sundarbans, making it extremely fertile. Due to the great river currents the east side of the Sundarbans is less saline and hence more lush than the western section. The Sundari trees grow here in abundance while on the western side quite different species of trees can be found.

The first historical record of any society inhabiting the region is of the 13th century when many Hindus, fleeing the Muslim advance, sought refuge amongst the forests. They settled here, building a number of palaces and temples. They were later joined by the Khiljis who were fleeing the Afghans. There are no other sign of early civilisations here. In the 17th century the Portuguese-Mogh pirates probably caused the population to quit the area although the lack of fresh drinking water and the unhealthy climate must have been other factors.

Since 1966 the Sundarbans has been a wildlife sanctuary and it is estimated that there are now 400 Royal Bengal Tigers and about 30 thousand spotted deer in the area. Besides its wildlife the Sundarbans has great economic potential. The Forest Departments keeps a close watch on the region and supervises activities to protect the delicate ecological balance. Hunting is prohibited.

Life in the Sundarbans

From November to mid-February thousands of fishermen from Chittagong converge on the island of Dhubla, on the mouth of the Kung or Masjat River, a Sundarbans estuary. They come with about 40 trawlers, each with 30 to 40 small boats in tow. During this period fishing is carried on ceaselessly, day and night. They reap the rich harvest of the schooling shrimps who come here to breed but also catch fish and sharks.

During the same period thousands of low-caste Hindus from Khulna, Barisal and Patuakhali come to the island for a three-day festival. They set up statues of deities in makeshift temples, bathe in the Ganges, and release or sacrifice goats. During the *mela* a fair is held with sweetmeats, dried fruits, toys, hookahs, wooden clogs and religious paraphernalia sold in the market. A few weeks after their departure the fishermen also head back to Chittagong and for the next nine months the island is deserted.

Fishing families who live like sea gypsies can also be seen in the Sundarbans. They have large boats with thatched roofs and cabins and they catch fish using trained otters. Nets are placed at the mouths of streams or creeks and the otters are then released up stream and chase the fish down into the nets.

Besides producing fish in great quantities, the region produces the Sundari tree which is in demand as a lightpole, for shipbuilding, railway sleepers, etc. Other forest products include honey, gol leaves, reeds and snails for lime. The honey-gatherers, who are known as *mauals*, constitute an occasional part of the diet of the Royal Bengal Tiger which is now re-establishing its once depleted numbers in the Sundarbans. The unfortunate *mauals* are a particular favourite of the tigers because they're always looking up at the trees. Other unique animals include the beautiful spotted deer. Birdlife not surprisingly matches the lushness of the jungle in its variety and numbers.

In the Satkhira Range the palace of Pratapaditya, one time overlord of the region, is one of the few man-made attractions of the region.

The Sundari Tree

The region derives its name from the Sundari trees that grow here to about 25 metres tall. The trees are very straight, have very tiny branches and keep well in water – they become rockhard when submerged for a long time. It is felled mainly for shipbuilding, electric poles, railway sleepers and house construction. Its wood has a purple lustre and accounts for about 75% of total wood extractions and exports. The gema wood, also felled in the Sundarbans, is mainly pulped for the Khulna newsprint factory. Timber workers here are called *bawalis*.

Royal Bengal Tigers

The Royal Bengal Tiger is the pride of Bangladesh. It was aptly named by the British for it grows to about four metres in length, is strong and considered to be the most majestic of tigers. It has a life span of 16 years and preys on deer, boars and fish stranded on riverbeds at low tide. It is only in old age, when they have lost their physical agility and their canine fangs, that they sometimes prey on workers in the area. Yearly about 25% become old and turn man-eater, particularly in April and May when it really begins to get warm and the Sundarbans hum with activity.

Other Wildlife

The spotted deer is considered the most beautiful in the world. They are easy to find for they come down to a clearing or to the riverbanks to drink. The monkeys here have been observed curiously dropping keora leaves whenever the deer appear on the scene.

Birdlife includes snipe, white and gold herons, woodcocks, common cranes, the golden eagle and the Madan-Tak – Adjutant Bird – which looks worried and dejected. Migratory birds are mainly ducks.

Economic Activity

On the southern fringes of the Sundarbans shrimp culture has recently developed extensively. Shrimp ponds can be seen here and lobsters are also caught. There are now cold storage centres where the fishermen can sell their catch. Thirty two patrol posts have been established, mainly to deal with smugglers in the ares. The main post is located in the Karam Jallal area.

Places to Stay

Heron Point (Nilkamal) is the only place you can stay; it is run by the Port Authority and is principally for their staff. The three-storey *Port Authority Staff House* has aircon rooms, a dining hall, bar and recreation facilities for the staff of about 30 and for visiting pilots. Tourist rates for the rooms are Tk 90 for singles, Tk 125 for doubles. There is no wildlife at Heron Point apart from birdlife and at night the only sound is the booming of waves.

Getting There & Away

As the Sundarbans are about 300 km south of Mongla with nothing in between, getting there and getting around is an expensive proposition. Hiring a motor boat ranges from Tk 1000 to 5000 for a round trip. There is some chance of hitching a ride with a Port Authority boat or Forest Officer going down to Heron Point, but hardly to be relied upon, and what's more you've got to be in Khulna or Mongla to start with. Another possibility is to hire a boat from the Forest Office in Dhangmari. Once you get to Heron Point you still have the problem of getting out into the Sundarbans. Only row boats are used to tour the hinterlands.

If you cannot get right down to Heron Point you can take local country boats about half way down, a distance of about 150 km. They carry large earthen pots of freshwater for the settlements on the edges of the dense jungle. The boats are pretty fast, speeding down with the ebb tide current early in the morning and bringing back a load of gol leaves or bundles of reeds with the incoming tide in the afternoon. The main problem is communicating with the boatmen who, to a man, know no English – apart from the word 'baksheesh'.

Parjatan Tourism conduct a guided package tour for a minimum party of 10 to the Sundarbans in winter. They also hire out transport to get there and they have land and water transport available in the Sundarbans. Contact the head office of Parjatan in Dacca for more information. For permits to visit the Sundarbans contact the Divisional Forest Officer (tel 20665) in Khulna.

BARISAL

A hundred km to the east of Khulna, Barisal is a district centre which houses the Cadet College of the Khulna Division, but not much else. There are a few jute mills but nothing of particular interest either for the business person or traveller. There are only two pre-Moghul mosques in the outlying districts. The one in the village of Qasba Guarnadi is nine-domed while the other is the single-domed mosque built in 1464 in the district of Patuakhali. There are apparently some newer Buddhist temples in Bakerganj and Patuakhali and there are medieval Hindu temples in the villages of Madubashah, Goyllah, Badajur and Bangaparipara.

The town originally developed near the ghats and is still relatively small and compact. Here you'll find old, low, ramshackle structures while the saddar area has the buildings of the British era, all looking grey and grimy with age.

To the south of Barisal on the Bay of Bengal there are apparently some fine beaches. It takes nine hours to get to Kuakata by launch. The lake at Madubashah, just 10 km from Barisal, is a bird sanctuary.

Places to Stay

The *Catholic Guesthouse* on Saddar St has just two rooms at Tk 10-20 for a bed. Check with the German father there. Near the large Anglican Church the Oxford Mission's *Douglas Boarding* is an old dark-red building. Four km out of town, beyond the College of Medicine, the *Oriental Institute* has rooms for Tk 75 with breakfast, tiffin and other meals included. A straight single is Tk 40 but food is rather expensive at this pleasantly peaceful place.

The *Hotel Bahadur* on Fazhul Haq Rd has singles/doubles at Tk 25/40 or with attached bathroom at Tk 30/50. On Agurpur Rd the *Hotel Melody* has similar standards and rates. The *Hotel Gulbagh* on Saddar Rd has rooms at Tk 20/40 or with attached bathroom at Tk 30/50. At 106 Chowk Bazar the *Hotel Islamia* is near the resthouse and the ferry ghats and has rooms from just Tk 15.

Finally the *Hotel Nurpur* (tel 3377) on Line Rd is the best in town with singles/doubles at Tk 60/100.

Places to Eat

The restaurant considered to be the best in town is adjacent to the Hotel Gulbagh and in the same building. Other eating places are in the ghat and bazar areas – they're basic but the food isn't bad.

Getting There & Away

River The most common method of transport to Barisal is by ferry or launch. To Khulna there are departures at 6 am for the 12-hour trip. To Mongla departures are also at 6 am and the trip takes 10 hours. Dacca departures are at 6 pm and the trip takes 12 hours. On Tuesdays and Fridays at 5.30 pm there are departures to Chittagong via Sondwip, Hatia, Dolata and Rangamati. Fares are:

	1st	2nd	Inter	3rd
Khulna	Tk 222	Tk 134	Tk 61	Tk 40
Mongla	Tk 164	Tk 99	Tk 45	Tk 30
Dacca	Tk 203	Tk 123	Tk 55	Tk 35
Chittagong	Tk 284	Tk 189	Tk 85	Tk 57

There are also launches to Dacca with fares of Tk 173 in 1st class or Tk 25 in deck class. The trip takes 12 to 14 hours. It is possible to get a ride on a cargo boat to Chittagong although reports say this can

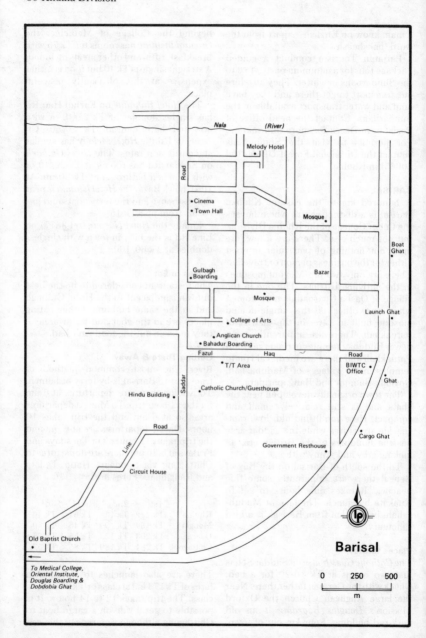

Nala (River)

Melody Hotel

Road

Cinema
Town Hall

Mosque

Boat Ghat

Gulbagh
Boarding

Bazar

Mosque

Launch Ghat

College of Arts

Anglican Church
Bahadur Boarding

Fazul   Haq   Road

T/T Area

BIWTC
Office

Ghat

Saddar

Catholic Church/Guesthouse

Hindu Building

Road

Line

Cargo Ghat

Government Resthouse

Circuit House

Barisal

Old Baptist Church

To Medical College,
Oriental Institute,
Douglas Boarding &
Dobdobia Ghat

0   250   500
m

be a fairly vicarious experience, especially when the cargo is being loaded/unloaded. This appears to be done with a notable lack of care and expertise – be careful or something heavy might land on your head. It takes about 20 hours to get to Chittagong despite the 12 hours scheduled.

Road & Rail There are road and rail links to Jessore but either trip is long and circuitous. The railway head is at Bhanga and the road route is via Faridpur. There is only a dirt track as well as several river crossings on the route to Jessore via Gopalganj and Bhatiapra Ghat. It's usually easier by ferry or launch.

Buses to Bakerganj, 12 km away, cost Tk 3.50. Patuakhali is 36 km distance and the fare is Tk 8. From Patuakhali there are buses to Barguna, Galachipa and Kebo Para.

RIVER TRIPS

A long river trip is one of the best experiences Bangladesh has to offer and the Khulna-Barisal-Dacca trip is a fine one. The BIWTC 'Rocket' ferry starts from Khulna at 6 am and arrives at Mongla at 8.30 am. It departs just 15 minutes later and goes upstream of the Mongla Nala. In this southern region of the Khulna division the rivers are wider, the islands wooded, interspersed with the usual rice paddies.

As usual the river life is busy – loaded barges are towed; large country boats lumber by with huge oars at the bow; sailboats have tattered sails, some of them so patched with multi-coloured pieces of cloth that they look like a quilt; and there's the usual 'black boats' with their usual country cargoes. As the 'Rocket' churns along heavily laden small boats rush to the riverbanks to avoid the wash, lightly laden boats take advantage of it to coast down the crests.

The large country boats are a fine sight. With their sails full up they can move at a fair speed but they generally also have a team of four to six men handling five-metre-long oars. The oars are so long the oarsmen must stand on a platform above the cabin. They do a sort of waltz, taking 2½ steps forward then turning round to push the oars back in the other direction.

The 'Rocket' is painted bright orange and is crowded despite its large size. The 1st and 2nd class cabins, the teashops and the dining hall are on the upper deck. Most of the deck class passengers lay out mats and bundles to reserve a piece of the lower deck for the trip, but others rent cabins from the crew. The lower decks are lively with cooking on improvised stoves, men playing card games, vendors hawking bananas, cigarettes, fried lentils with onions, peanuts or betelnut 'pan'. Other passengers lean on iron railings or sit on boxes to watch the river scenery.

It takes 3½ hours to Moralganj, the first stop. Some stops have ghats with a floating barge in front, others have no docking facilities at all but there is always a crowd of rivercraft. From Moralganj another three hours takes the ferry to Ghularhat and then it's two hours to Jhalaghati and 1½ hours to Barisal where the boat arrives at dusk. Again the stop is short but the smaller rivercraft are already stopping along the riverbanks as the 'Rocket' leaves for the overnight trip to Dacca. Dawn the next morning sees you arriving in the capital.

River Gypsies

Bangladesh's river gypsies, the Badhi or Badhja, make up about 50% of the riverboat people of the country and are mainly low-caste Hindus. They move as a clan from one river to another, selling herbal medicine and jewellery which includes the pink pearls they gather from river oysters. During the monsoon when the river swells and extends the navigable rivers to outlying villages they scatter out to the countryside to trade but in winter they move down to their usual havens like Mirpur, Savar and the Dhakeswari Rivers.

Their houseboats are very tidy, neat and clean with shelves for garments, bedding, pots and pans. Each houseboat houses a family, generally with just two or three children because of the limited space on the boats. The river gypsies include few elderly folk. They live their whole lives afloat but progress, even in Bangladesh, is starting to number their days. Motorised vessels, manufactured jewellery and modern medicine have made their inroads and some now send their children to schools. Still modernisation is a slow process in Bangladesh, it's likely to be a long long time before they disappear.

FARIDPUR

This is a small town with a number of old Hindu temples. The largest is the Orakandi Temple, located in the centre of town. Faridpur is also the hometown of the father of the nation, Sheikh Mujibur Rahman. On his birthday each year he was presented with thirty or forty thousand cattle – making him one of the wealthiest men in the land.

Places to Stay

The *Hotel Luxury* (tel 2623) at Goal Chamot has shops, a TV room and a restaurant. Rooms with attached bath cost Tk 25-40 for singles, Tk 45-75 for doubles.

Rajshahi Division

As the north-western division of the country, Rajshahi's borders are, as is usual, the major rivers; the Jamuna separates it from the Dacca Division while the Ganges/Padma borders the Khulna Division. The Ganges becomes very wide where it enters Bangladesh, stretching almost 20 km from bank to bank. The border with the Indian state of West Bengal is partially made by the Ganges, but for the most part it is an arbitrary line through thick jungle, sometimes marked by barbed-wire fences. Rajshahi stretches from the wooded *terai* region at the foothills of the Himalaya to the north right down to the broad Gangetic Valley to the south.

Vedic literature mentions the region as being inhabited by various tribes and being named *Varendra*. In the 4th century BC the Greeks fought with an Indian contingent called the Bangalas here. Bangala is a term which originated from the traditional building practice now know as *dolmanchar*, the construction of thatched bamboo huts called *bangala*, because of the design of the grass roof. With the emergence of the Mauryan Empire in the 3rd century BC and its

expansion under the Buddhist Emperor Ashoka the region became Buddhist and brick buildings, mainly of a religious character, were introduced.

The Mauryans were followed by the Bactrian-Greeks, the Scythians, Parthians and the Kushans who established the Gandhara Empire in the 1st century AD. Under the Kushans the silk trade flourished and carried Buddhism with it as far as the north of China. Pundravardhana, the old Buddhist Mauryan capital, became not only a Buddhist centre but also an important commercial entrepot of the silk trade. In turn the Kushans were swept aside by the Sassanians and in the 4th century AD the Guptas emerged and managed to retain their empire east of the Indus until the 6th century.

Pundravardhana must have continued to be the capital of Bangala until the 8th century. It was visited by Fa Hsien in the 5th century and Xuan Zhang two centuries later – both were impressed by the large monasteries inhabited by thousands of bhikkus, the soaring temples and the Ashoka stupas. When the Gupta empire finally disappeared the Harsha dynasty and then the Palas emerged and this region became the last stronghold of Buddhism on the subcontinent. Xuan Zhang found temples in Pundravardhana, Mainimati and Noakhali but he made no mention of Somapuri Vihara in Paharpur, which probably was built later. During the 8th century this division was the site for one of the most glorious regimes in the history of the Pala Kings of Bengal; (*Rajshahi* means 'the Royal Territory').

The Pala kingdom fell into poverty and Pundravardhana declined with the arrival of the Senas in the 12th century. They moved their capital down to the Maldah area in Gaur where they stayed until the Turkestan Khiljis of Mohammed Bakhtiar booted them out in the 13th century. The thriving Hindu community had built temples of lavishly ornate design like the temples of India in the 8th and 9th centuries but under the Senas a simple indigenous temple design was adopted and followed through to the 12th century.

With the advent of Muslim power mosques began to be constructed. Their central Asian appearance – walled around with a single entrance and topped by a low dome – later took on an indigenous aspect when the *bangala* was made into a symbolic decorative piece on the top of mosques, just as it had been earlier on the roof of Hindu temples. The mosque in Kushuma is a good example while smaller mosques, like the Mazhar of Shaha Mukdum, used the traditional Bangala structural design.

More dynasties followed, the Afghans briefly replaced the Tuglukhs from 1520-76 but they moved their capital from Gaur (Lakhnauti under the Senas) to Sonargaon. The Moghuls too moved from Rajshahi to Dacca but they were to make Rajmahal above the Ganges their capital for sometime, until it was finally moved to Murshidabad.

The British, like everywhere in Bangladesh, were the most efficient in the development of natural resources and Rajshahi under their control was quickly turned into a sugar and cotton-producing region. Today Rajshahi is the centre of the country's sericulture and silk industry. The British also divided the region into two districts, Rajshahi in the south and Bogra in the north. It was also in this division that the first anti-British rumblings, the *Farassi-Sanyassin Movement*, arose in the latter part of the 18th century.

The archaeological sites in this division are quite dazzling for their range. It is, however, an area which is as yet undeveloped for the tourist trade, and consequently many of these sites are sitting in the middle of grainfields or villages, just waiting for somebody to take an interest in them. Economically Rajshahi, apart from the Rangpur region in the north, is one of the better off areas of the country.

BOGRA DISTRICT

Bogra is a small district, having only a single sub-division, Jaipurhat, which is now becoming a district. The whole district is given over to the production of cotton and sugar, though there is movement afoot to exploit the coal and limestone deposits. The district is also known for its high-quality sweetmeats, yoghurt and particularly for its archaeological sites.

BOGRA

Bogra is an old town that seems to have only just begun to recognise the changes taking place in the world. As a central road junction it gets a fairly heavy concentration of transient visitors, but hardly any stay longer than necessary.

The town itself is interesting only for its Hindu temples, mosques, and remaining British architecture, set amongst a maze of narrow paved lanes. In an attempt to stimulate interest in the district's industries a winter fair is held here each year. The town bridges still show the scars left by the war of 1971 – they remain unrepaired.

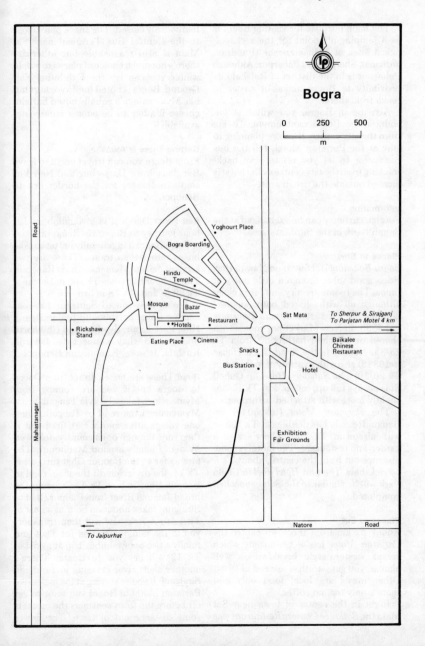

Bogra

0   250   500
m

Yoghourt Place

Bogra Boarding

Hindu Temple

Mosque

Bazar

Rickshaw Stand

Hotels

Restaurant

Sat Mata

To Sherpur & Sirajganj
To Parjatan Motel 4 km

Eating Place   Cinema

Snacks

Baikalee Chinese Restaurant

Bus Station

Hotel

Road

Mahastanagar

Exhibition Fair Grounds

Natore   Road

To Jaipurhat

The main purpose for visiting Bogra is as a jumping-off point for the archaeological sites of Mahastanagar (Pundravardhana), Sherpur and Paharpur. Although Paharpur is in the district of Rajshahi its proximity to Bogra makes it easier to reach from there.

Arriving in Bogra, you will first encounter the Bogra cantonment, 10 km from the city centre. If you're planning to stay at the Parjatan Motel, tell the bus conductor to let you off to save backtracking from the city centre as the hotel is located outside the urban area.

Information
Foreign currency can be exchanged at the Sonali Bank in the Sat Mata area.

Places to Stay
Bogra Boarding (tel 5609) on Nawab Bari Rd is good value though a little noisy at times. The rooms are airy and fairly clean although all with shared bath, singles/doubles are Tk 15/24. *Janata Boarding* (tel 6883) in New Market has rooms with shared or attached bathrooms from Tk 25/35. Nearby is the *Azad Guest House* (tel 6342) also with a variety of rooms from Tk 20/30. The *Saleheen Hotel* on Guhail St is always full up; rooms cost Tk 15/35, slightly more with attached bathroom.

The *Parjatan Motel* (tel 5044) on Banani Rd only has doubles at Tk 100 or with aircon at Tk 200. There's also a garden and restaurant. The motel is some distance out from the centre, about Tk 5 by rickshaw. The new *Hotel Joel* in Chalo Park will be similar to the Saleheen when completed.

Places to Eat
About six km from the town centre the *Parjatan Motel* has a restaurant which serves western-style breakfasts – well almost, you get parathas instead of toast. Other meals are local food only and there's only tea, no coffee.

Right in the centre of town near Sat Mata the *Baikalee Chinese Restaurant* was temporarily closed. The snack place close to the Central Bus Terminal near Sat Mata is also reasonable but otherwise there's not much choice of places to eat. In winter you can try the Exhibition Fair Ground. Bogra is noted for its yoghurt but like Mymensingh's equally noted buffalo-cheese it's like to be *paowa jaina* – not available!

Getting There & Away
From Bogra you can travel north to leave Bangladesh for Darjeeling and Nepal or south to Jessore for the border exit to Benopol.

Rail From Dacca it is a roundabout 12-hour journey to Bogra via Rangpur.

From Bogra it is generally better to take buses rather than trains. There are two services daily to Mymensingh via Rangpur. The 12 hour trip costs Tk 160 in 1st class, Tk 39 in 2nd, Tk 18 in 3rd.

Trains also run to Santahar for connecting trains northbound to Jamalganj, Hilli, Parbatipur, Syedpur and Chiliharti. Southbound they connect to Ishurdi, Kushtia, Jessore, Khulna and Benopol.

Road There are buses direct from Dacca to Bogra but if you are coming from Mymensingh take a bus via Tangail. From Mymensingh the road to Tangail is just one village after another at first; but it then runs through open country, followed by dense jungle around Madhupur. The fare as far as the Baopur Ghat turn-off is Tk 14, the diversion off the main road to Baopur Ghat is just Tk 1. Crossing the broad Jamuna River from Baopur Ghat to Sirajgunj takes about an hour at a cost of Tk 1.50. A rickshaw will then transport you to the minibus station for Tk 4 and finally a two hour minibus trip at a cost of Tk 12 will get you to Bogra. There's another short river crossing just outside Sirajgunj. If you're staying at the expensive Parjatan Motel in Bogra you want to get off before the town centre as the motel is some distance out of town. The newer buildings of Bogra's cantonment commences a full 10 km before you arrive in the town centre.

From Dacca the route is via Aricha, the road running on an elevated causeway one to four metres above the general ground level. During the monsoon all this surrounding area is flooded. The trip to Aricha takes a little over two hours but the ghat here serves two ferry terminals on the west bank of the Jamuna and the Padma and this is the biggest river bottleneck in the whole country. Ferries depart from here for Nagarbari for traffic going to Rajshahi and for Daulatdia for those going to Khulna. A bridge is being planned which will ease the delays.

From Bogra's Central Bus Terminal there are departures from 5.30 am to 3 pm. Dacca buses leave hourly and take eight or nine hours at a fare of Tk 32. BRTC buses cost Tk 49. Travel times depend on that lengthy ferry crossing at Aricha.

Buses to Rajshahi go via Natore. There are also services to Ishurdi and Pabna. Northbound buses to Rangpur take 2½ hours and cost Tk 12.50. They also go to Jaipurhat and Santahar.

AROUND BOGRA

The main purpose of going to Bogra is to visit the archaeological sites of Mahastanagar, Sherpur and Paharpur nearby.

MAHASTANAGAR

Mahastanagar is identified with the ancient city of Pundravardhana, the oldest capital of Bangala, which dates from the Mauryan Empire (3rd century BC). Located 16 km from Bogra in the Bogra district, it was the principal seat of administration until the 15th century. The ruins of the city are partly excavated and can be seen by tourists. There is a museum attached to the site which is worth visiting. The site is historically significant but archaeologically poor.

Museum

The museum is 1½ km from Mahastanagar. The archaeological remains are mainly made up of old bricks which form the foundations on both sides of the paved road. The museum is on the left with the Archaeological Resthouse just across on the right. The museum has a lovely large garden with carved stone archways taken from the site at Sherpur. Artifacts include carved stones, terracotta toys, earthen pots and coins, including square ones dating back to the 2nd and 3rd centuries BC. The museum is open from 9 am to 5 pm.

Vasu Vihara

This is the major archaeological site, situated on rolling hills 12 km to the northwest of Mahastanagar. In the 7th century AD the Buddhist traveller Xuan Zhang wrote of this site as accommodating 700 monks in the monasteries, and noted the gigantic Ashoka stupa. Today all that remains are the brickwork foundations; impressive for their breadth rather than height.

A rickshaw ride will cost Tk 6 or 7 from town. En route you cross a river where you can see men fishing with cumbersome nets framed by long bamboo poles and youngsters laboriously transferring water into irrigation channels using heavy wooden troughs.

Behollah Lakindar

This site is eight km away on the Mahastanagar road. Get off at Gakul and walk three km to the west from the main road, or take one of the rickshaws which will be waiting here. There is apparently a palace where the son of a nawab of the area was bitten by a snake sent by Pada Devi, the mystic fakir; but then again, there could be nothing at all . . . .

Places to Stay

There is a *Parjatan Inn*, the only concrete structure in the area, should you wish to stay. There's no one here except for the chowkidar, a helpful, friendly fellow who could arrange a rickshaw for you if you want to explore some of the minor sites nearby. Dorm beds are Tk 15, singles/doubles Tk 50/100 but there is no eating place around here.

Getting There

Buses and minibuses run from the Central Bus Terminal in Bogra to Mahastanagar and cost Tk 3. There are also babytaxis from a lane off the main roadway, they cost Tk 5. You could take a rickshaw but it would be much more expensive.

SHERPUR

Sherpur is 16 km south of Bogra and was the first site of a Hindu kingdom. It has some of the more intact archaeological remains of this region. Not much has been dug up as of yet so there is little knowledge of the history and archaeology of the area.

In the village of Sherpur is the Mazhar of Khalogaji and nearby is the three-domed Keruah Mosque of 1582. The Mazhar of Shah Bandigiri Shah is in the traditional Moghul-Bangala architectural style.

PAHARPUR

The Somapuri Vihara at Paharpur is the biggest Buddhist monastery south of the Himalaya and dates from the 8th century. It is so impressive that it was declared a protected archaeological site in 1919 although the scholar-traveller Dr Buckman Hamilton had shown his interest in it as far back as 1807-12. The Buddhist temple at Lauriya Nandangarh in north Bihar state in India appears to have been the architectural prototype. It differs only in that the wall base is embellished with terracotta artwork.

A large amount of money has been set aside for the development of this area as a tourist site, but given the speed at which things happen in Bangladesh it could be a few more years before the peace and beauty are disturbed.

Somapuri Vihara

The temple is in the shape of a large quadrangle covering 11 hectares with the monks' cells making up the walls and enclosing a courtyard. From the centre of the courtyard rises a 20-metre-high temple which dominates the whole countryside. There's a good view from the very top of the structure. The temple measure about 300 metres square and its cruciform floor plan is topped by a three-tier super-structure with the first raised just slightly above ground level. The second rises almost three times higher and the third level soars up to be topped by a large, hollow, square cubicle somewhat similar to the hollow tower structure of Moenjodaro in Pakistan.

This *Mahavihara* or large monastery has slightly recessed walls embellished with very well preserved terracotta bas-reliefs of rural folk and wildlife in their local settings. The clay tiles are not sequentially arranged – they were really meant to be admired individually as decorative pieces and not to tell a story. The monastic cells, more than 170 in all, are quite small and of these 72 have ornamental pedestals in the centre the purpose of which still eludes archaeologists. It is possible they contained the remains of saintly monks who had been in residence in these cells. The cells have a drainage system with 22 outlets to the courtyard, marked by stone gargoyles.

There are points of interest on each side of the courtyard. On the east side you can make out the outline of what was once a miniature model of the temple. On the western wing of the north side are the remains of structures the purpose of which continues to baffle archaeologists. On the eastern wing of the south side is an elevated brickwork with an eight-pointed star-shaped structure which must have been a shrine. The remains a little to the west appear to have been the monk's refectory and kitchen.

Except for the guardhouse to the north most of the remains outside the courtyard

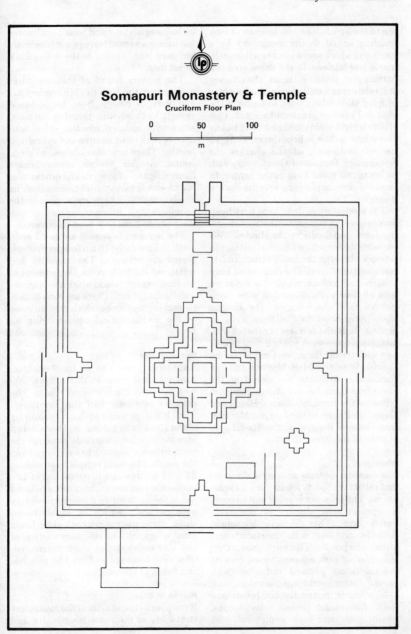

Somapuri Monastery & Temple

Cruciform Floor Plan

0   50   100

m

are to the south. They include an oblong building linked to the monastery by a causeway which may have been the wash-house and latrines. In the same area is a bathing ghat, probably Hindu. The villagers still relate that Sandhyavata, the daughter of King Mahidahan, used to bathe at the ghat and became pregnant by a god. This Hindu legend seems to spring up in nearly every lake in the subcontinent! Only 12 metres south-west of the ghat is the rectangular Temple of Gondeswari with an octagonal pillar base in the centre. In front is a circular platform seven metres in diameter.

The monastery is thought to have been successively occupied by the Buddhists, the Jains, and finally by the Hindus. This explains the sometimes curious mixture in artwork although the basic structure has remained unaltered. The Jains must have constructed a *chaturmukhar*, a structure with all four walls decorated with stone bas-reliefs of their deities. The Hindus made alterations to the base walls to replace Buddhist terracotta artwork with sculptural stonework of their own deities and with terracotta artwork representing themes from the Mahabharata and the Ramayana. Artifacts discovered at the site range from bronze statues and bas reliefs of the elephant-headed Hindu god Ganesh to statues of the Jain god Manzuri; from bronze images of the Buddha to statues of the infant Krishna.

Museum

The museum contains an array of domestic and religious objects found during excav-ations. The museum is small and has only a representative display of the items found here. They include household utensils, grinding mills, mortars, curry stones and pestles. There are also earthen pots, clay saucers, ink-pots, vases, cooking vessels (some painted and some with carved designs), oil lamps, stone statues, stucco heads, terracotta bas-reliefs and balls, flat round tablets, clay stupas, beads, seals and toys. Sculptural work

includes sandstone and basalt sculptures but the stonework of Hevagara in passionate embrace with Shakti is the collection's finest item.

The pottery found at the site dates mainly from the 10th to 12th century AD and vary in design from broad-based vessels to those with tapering bottoms, some with spouted mouths, other with narrow necks and mouths and cylindrical bodies. There are also dishes, saucers, lamps, circular vessels, nude female figures, figures of animals and ornamental bricks with floral patterns. Stucco Buddha heads unearthed here are similar to the Gandhara style. Some copper plates with inscriptions have also been discovered.

The museum is open 9 am to 12 noon and 2 to 5 pm daily; 10 am to 5 pm Fridays; closed on holidays. The museum and resthouse are both in the Department of Archaeology compound which also encloses a well kept garden. There are storehouses behind the resthouse which contain most of the archaeological artifacts dug up here.

Satyapir Vita

Approaching the site on the Jamalganj road you first come to this temple, 400 metres east of the Somapuri Vihara. The complex originally had the Temple of Tara. It is trapezoidal in shape, measuring about 75 x 40 x 85 metres, and is walled up except on the northern side although the main entrance appears to have been from the south. The main temple is an oblong 24 x 12 metres and is composed of two parts – the sanctum in the north, a pillared hall in the south with a circumnambulatory passage, and a shrine. A square-based stupa, three metres on each side, has a small reliquary. The reliquary was full of tiny clay votive stupas when discovered, they were apparently offered by pilgrims as a token of reverence.

Places to Stay

If you plan to spend a day at the monastery start early as the place is extensive and fascinating. There is a spartan *Archaeological Rest House* with two rooms costing just Tk 15 plus Tk 10 for water, which has to be fetched. You may be able to buy some food here to have prepared but it's advisable to bring supplies with you. The custodian is a kindly and friendly fellow who may invite you to have tea with him.

Getting There
From Bogra Paharpur is 56 km west of Bogra. First take a bus or minibus to Jaipurhat, 44 km away. It is a 2½ hour trip costing Tk 8 by bus, Tk 10 by minibus. From this developing little sugar-producing town take a train for the short 15-minute trip north to the village of Jamalganj. Finally it's a five-km walk through the countryside to Paharpur.

From Jaipurhat There is an alternative route from Jaipurhat to Paharpur but it's somewhat complicated. You first have to travel seven km west to Dugrahador, from there it is four km over a broken brick road to Kochnapur where you leave the road and follow the bunds between paddy fields. You really need a guide for the two km from here to the actual village of Kochnapur from where it is another three km to the Paharpur site.

From Rajshahi It is also possible to get there from Rajshahi, in which district Paharpur actually lies. From Rajshahi it is almost 100 km north via Naogaon, which is just 28 km from Paharpur. From Naogaon it is 20 km to Badolgazhi and from this village there is no transport for the final eight km to Paharpur. This is not a very good route unless you plan to overnight at Paharpur.

RANGPUR
The Research Centre for Leprosy is located here. Apart from this highlight there are minor Buddhist archaeological sites in the outlying villages of Nilfumarcy and Birat. It is principally a transit point to more important towns like Bogra, Dinajpur, Chiliharti, Lalmanirhat and Syedpur. Fine quality jute and canvas carry bags are made in Rangpur.

Places to Stay & Eat
There are a few hotels such as the *Oasis Resthouse* on Central Rd which has rooms with and without attached bathroom from Tk 13/36. The *Sittara Resthouse* on Gupta Rd has similar standards and rates.

The choice of eating places in Rangpur is extremely limited.

Getting There & Away
There are buses and trains between Rangpur and Dinajpur, Chiliharti or Dacca. By road or rail you can travel between Dacca and Rangpur via Mymensingh, crossing the river either at Bahadurabad Ghat to Fulekari Ghat (a two-hour crossing) or further north at Chilmari. If you are going to the extreme north of the division it is better to take the train as delays at Aricha for bus travellers can be so long. From Rangpur buses go to Syedpur every half hour, the one-hour trip costs Tk 5.

DINAJPUR
Dinajpur, 70 km to the west of Rangpur, is a quiet provincial town, enlivened only by the arrival of a bus or train. Larger, and by relative standards more sophisticated than Rangpur, Dinajpur has come to grips with the 20th century to such an extent that it has pulled down the only medieval mosque in the town and replaced it with a glittering new one. Denuded of this solitary object of interest, Dinajpur is not a highpoint.

The Shuja Mosque on Station Rd has also recently been demolished. This small brick mosque of Bangala-Moghul style was built in 1804 and was noted as a landmark by Cyril Radcliffe at the time of partition.

Information
The Sonali Bank on Nimtole Rd exchanges

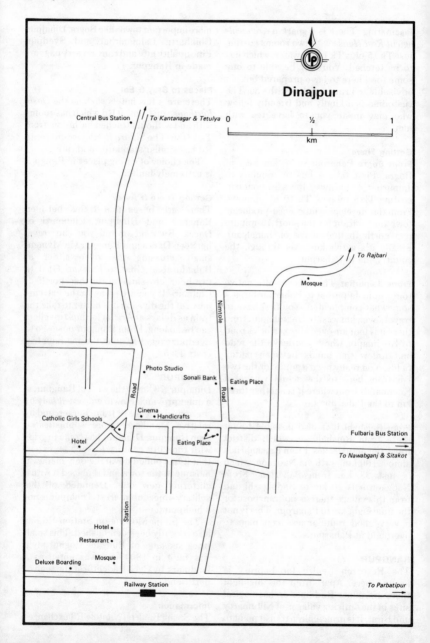

Dinajpur

foreign currency and is open 9 am to 1 pm. The Unmesh Handicraft Display Centre on the main street, near the Cinema Modern, offers a small range of handicrafts – mainly textiles and ceramic products.

Places to Stay & Eat

The *Hotel Nobina* in Bahadur Bazar off Station Rd has singles/doubles with shared bath for Tk 25/40. It compares favourably with the *Hotel Rehana* on Station Rd which has rooms at the same price. Also on Station Rd *Deluxe Boarding* has basic shared bathroom singles/doubles for Tk 12/20.

The *New Hotel* on Station Rd is the best in town with singles/doubles for Tk 40/70. It also has an adjacent restaurant which can be described as the best in town. Other than that Dinajpur's eating places are pretty basic. There are no Chinese restaurants here.

Getting There & Away

Rail Trains run north to Pachagar, east only to Parbatipur from where trains connect to the south. There are three trains daily and the half hour trip costs Tk 3 in 3rd class. Connecting trains to Chiliharti only go via Syedpur. You may have to wait some time for a train there – the quickest way out is to take a bus to Rangpur and another to Bogra. If you are heading to Rajshahi or south, however, the trains are better since they are broad gauge.

Parbatipur is the largest railway junction in the Rajshahi division, from here to Natore is 156 km. The 3½ hour trip costs Tk 94 in 1st, Tk 28 in 2nd, Tk 7 in 3rd. The railway runs pretty close to the Indian border. From Natore minibuses take 1½ hours to make the 48-km trip to Rajshahi, the fare is Tk 10.

Road to Dacca The Dacca-Dinajpur trip takes about 12 hours by BRTC bus at a fare of Tk 82.

Road to Tetulya The undulating road to Tetulya is one of the most scenic in Bangladesh. It runs through Takurgaon, 64 km away, which is known for sugar and high grade tobacco. Along the way is a water tank covering about 2½ square km. It was built in the 8th century by the Pala dynasty.

The Tetulya border crossing to India is now closed, however. The Chiliharti crossing is the only one open in this north-west area.

AROUND DINAJPUR

Rajbari

Only four km from Dinajpur this old maharajah's palace is now in ruins but there is a well kept Hindu temple with an attractively painted archway. The palace, designed by somebody who was determined to demonstrate an eclectic and travelled mind, is built in a baroque style, complete with Greek columns and pediments. It dates from the 18th century. The imposing main archway leads to another, topped by a brightly painted stone lion. Through this gate is yet another archway to the Hindu temple or *mandir*. The entrances from the wall on the right lead to an overgrown courtyard and the palace.

Getting There A rickshaw costs Tk 5 in each direction.

Kantanagar Temple

This is a perfect example of the indigenous design of Hindu temples of the medieval period. It dates from 1454 and is 26 km from Dinajpur.

The temple is enclosed by high walls, but an entrance is to be found to the right from the road. Overall, the temple follows the familiar fortified design, with the cells for the monks ringing the building. The inner courtyard contains the temple, kept clean and freshly painted although parts of the terracotta frieze that covered the entire wall from top to bottom are broken. The temple was built during the period of the Khiljis Muslims who had their capital in old Gaur and there is just a hint of Turkish influence in the design. The area must have been a minor rajbari but no trace of a palace remains.

There is much similarity in both style and structure between this temple and the Paharpur edifice: both are three-tiered and have the sides decorated with terracotta artwork. The artwork, however, is more refined here, portraying the usual stories from the Mahabharata and Ramayana together with the various Hindu deities from the base of the walls up to the cornice that defines the second level. This also has arched windows and pillars and over the third tier is the curved Bangala roof, usually placed as a decorative piece. It has no functional purpose as it is too small, the real roof protrudes like a canopy.

Getting There To get there take a bus from the Central Bus Terminal and tell the conductor where you want to go. Get off the bus in Kantanagar village where it may or may not stop – remind the conductor after about 20 km. The fare is Tk 3. From the road a dirt track goes left through the village and down to the river, from where you can see the temple's rooftop with the peculiar Bangala curvilinear roof design. A bamboo footbridge crosses the river; it's a fair walk to the temple but the scenery is pleasantly rural.

Sitakot

Since 1968 excavations at Sitakot, 46 km north-east of Dinajpur in the area of Nawabganj and only a few km away from Charkai Railway Station, have exposed a Buddhist monastery from the 7th to 8th century. A hurried survey of the area revealed 50 similar ancient mounds, though many have been damaged by locals hunting for bricks.

The monastery was built on a square plan and the 40 living spaces for monks once overlooked a central courtyard. Several Bodhisattva images were un-

covered during excavations but nothing remains except for traces of the foundations.

Getting There Buses go from the Fulbaria Bus Station and cost Tk 8, minibuses cost Tk 10.

Sura Mosque

The Sura Mosque is in the upazila of Goraghat, 62 km north-east of Dinajpur. Built between 1493 and 1538 this pre-Moghul brick-and-stone mosque has walls covered with geometrically designed stone carvings. The single high bulbous dome covers the main sanctuary. The ornamentation is lavish and the style similar to the Chotta Shona Mosque in Gaur. It's difficult to find as practically no one appears to know about it.

Getting There Buses and minibuses go from the Fulbaria Bus Station and cost Tk for a bus, Tk 12 for a minibus.

Ramshagar Lake

This picnic spot is eight km out of Dinajpur and has boating and angling facilities. There is no public transport, so rickshaws or autorickshaws are the only way to get there.

RAJSHAHI DISTRICT

One of the oldest regions of Bangladesh, Rajshahi is now most noted for its production of sugarcane, which is as important here as tea is in Sylhet. The presence of the Gupta and Palas dynasties up to the 12th century has left a legacy of ancient and medieval ruins of considerable interest and in a good state of preservation. It remained the capital of Bangala under the Khiljis and later the Afghans until the 17th century but the Moghuls, who ruled here later, attached very little importance to the district except as a strategic buffer zone although they established it as the capital of a *subha* or province. After Dacca became unsafe they moved their capital to Rajmahal but as maritime commerce shifted more and more to Calcutta they finally moved their capital to Murshidabad.

As usual the British saw its economic potential and developed the region. They established their capital in Rajshahi, the city from which the whole division takes its name.

RAJSHAHI

Though some distance from the mainstream of traffic through Bangladesh, Rajshahi is by no means a backwater. It has the usual quota of British and post-independence buildings, giving the town a very apparent sense of history.

Located on the north bank of the Ganges, the town is protected by a high dyke from monsoonal flooding. The Farakka Barrage in India controls the flow of the Ganges – during winter hardly any water flows through here. The British section of the town was built around the edges of the old city; the space in between became the *saddar*, the modern part of the city.

The city has a museum, housed in an attractive, old building known as the Varendra, which has a research department concerned with the ancient history and culture of the region. The displays ranges from pre-history from around 3000 BC right up to the 18th century. The attractive building has lovely gardens but the displays spill out into the hallways and on to the courtyards.

On the outskirts of the city on the road to Natore are the Rajshahi University, the Colleges of Medicine, Engineering and Agriculture, the modern mosques, the radio station and the jute mills. Also located here is the Sericulture Research Institute as this is the main silk-growing region in the country. Rajshahi has a 600 hectare silkworm rearing area. The Sericulture Display Centre on Station Rd has various silk goods on display.

Information
The tourist office (tel 2392) is in the Parjatan Motel.

Places to Stay – bottom end
Padma Boarding in Shaheb Bazar near the Hotel Rajmahal has very simple rooms at Tk 12/20. The *Hotel Rajmahal* (tel 2785) on Shaheb Bazar Rd is good value with singles with attached bath from Tk 20 on the ground floor, Tk 27-32 upstairs. Doubles are Tk 36-45.

The *Hotel Moon* in Shaheb Bazar in the Ghoramora area has shared bath singles at Tk 22-30, doubles at Tk 36-45. *Hotel Gulshan* on Station Rd has only rooms with shared bath, they cost Tk 18/27 on the ground floor, Tk 20/30 upstairs.

Places to Stay – top end
The *Parjatan Motel* (tel 2392) on Abdul Majid Rd is behind a small Catholic church and has a restaurant and bar. Rooms cost Tk 75/100 or with aircon doubles are Tk 200. Suites are Tk 150 or Tk 250 with aircon.

Places to Eat
The *Nanking Chinese Restaurant* and the *Shantung Restaurant* are both on the Nawabganj Rd. They're often open later than the official hours of 11 am to 3 pm and 6 to 10 pm and the food here is quite good. The *Red Dragon Chinese Restaurant* on Malapara St is opposite the Telephone & Telegraph office. It's run by locals and has fairly good food although, as usual, only tea is available, no coffee.

The *Parjatan Motel Restaurant* on Abdul Majid Rd serves western-style breakfasts and local, Chinese and western meals. The bar has beer (for Tk 50) and other drinks. There are a few eating places around the Saheb Bazar – breakfast is paratha, halva and tea and is good value.

Getting There & Away
Air Biman has flights from Dacca on Tuesday, Thursday and Sunday and the fare is Tk 275. The Biman office (tel 2193) is at Sagarpara, Ghoramora. The airport is at Noahatai, eight km from town.

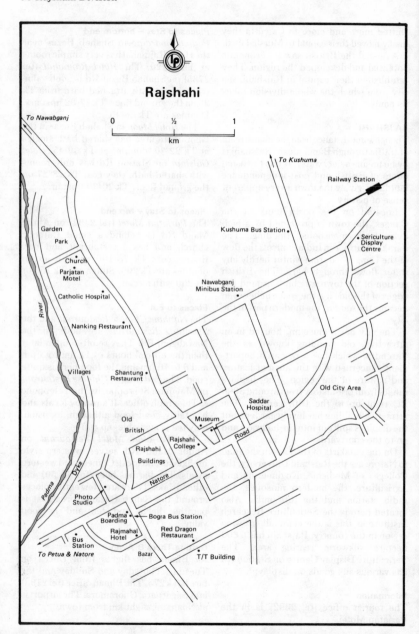

Rajshahi

To Nawabganj

0   ½   1
km

To Kushuma

Railway Station

Garden
Park

Church
Parjatan
Motel

Catholic Hospital

Nanking Restaurant

River

Kushuma Bus Station

Sericulture
Display
Centre

Nawabganj
Minibus Station

Villages

Shantung
Restaurant

Old City Area

Saddar
Hospital

Old
British

Museum

Rajshahi
College

Road

Rajshahi
Buildings

Natore

Dyke

Padma

Photo
Studio

Padma
Boarding

Bogra Bus Station

Rajmahal
Hotel

Red Dragon
Restaurant

Bus
Station

To Petua & Natore

Bazar

T/T Building

Top: Paharpur Temple, Paharpur, Rajshahi Division (BPC)
Bottom: terracotta friezes, Paharpur Temple, Paharpur, Rajshahi Division (JRS)

Top: Tole Holy Temple, Petu Rajbari, Rajshahi, Rajshahi Division (JRS)
Bottom: front wall of Grinda Temple, Rajshahi, Rajshahi Division (JRS)

River An interesting alternative route to Dacca is to go down to Khulna and take a ferry from there to Dacca.

Rail Trains to Dacca go via Santahar and Natore, from where you have to take a minibus. Buses are the fastest and most comfortable way. Via Mymensingh trains take 16 hours to Dacca.

Road From Dacca buses for Rajshahi go via Aricha (where there is a ferry crossing), Pabna and Ishurdi. The trip takes about 10-12 hours, depending on delays at Aricha, and costs Tk 66. If you cannot find a through bus it's just as easy to take a bus to Pabna and a connecting bus from there. From Pabna buses go to Ishurdi, Natore and Bogra or even further west to Rajshahi. Dacca buses from Rajshahi depart from the Shaheb Bazar every two hours from 6 am.

From Rajshahi to Ishurdi is 96 km via Natore, get off at the Dashuria road junction before Pabna for the Ishurdi minibus. It's Tk 15 to the junction and a further Tk 1 to Ishurdi. In Sailkupa, a town off the main highway between Ishurdi and Kaliganj, the medieval Jami Mosque is of a unique design with four towers.

If coming from Jessore the route is by rail or road – by rail to Ishurdi through Abdulpur to Rajshahi. There is no direct train connection so you have to change in Abdulpur whereas by bus you can travel direct from Ishurdi to Rajshahi. Travelling to Jessore or Khulna if you miss the last bus or the 4 pm train you can take a babytaxi for Tk 5 to the ferry ghat and across the river get another babytaxi to Kushtia for Tk 7. From here buses run to Jessore and less frequently to Khulna. Kushtia-Jessore costs Tk 15 for the 2½ to three hour trip. Alternatively the midnight express departs around 12.30 am and arrives in Jessore at 5.30 am, in Khulna at 6.30-7 am.

AROUND RAJSHAHI
Mazhar of Shaha Mukdum

Twelve km along the road to Natore is the Mazhar of Shaha Mukdum in typical Bangala architectural style. It is painted in the same bright greens and yellows typical of mosques in Pakistan.

Getting There A bus costs Tk 2.75 from Rajshahi.

Rajbari of Petua

A couple of km further towards Natore, just under a km from the main road via a dirt track, is this group of Hindu temples of a peculiar but attractive design. The Shiva temple is about 1200 years old, complete with stone carvings and sculptural works, which unfortunately were disfigured during the war of liberation. The temple is very ornate, with three tiers gradually tapering up and topped by a dome.

Nearby is the Temple of Wrath, dedicated to Radha-Krishna, the consort of Krishna. The temple guide and his family live underneath. The Tole Temple, also nearby, is of an entirely different style to the others. At the other end of the large open ground in front of the temple is the two-storey palace of the maharajah. It was built in 1895 by Rajah Naran Shanul and has now been turned into a college. Behind the palace are temples covered with terracotta friezes of gods and events from the Mahabharata and the Ramayana. The main one is the Grinda Temple.

Kusumba Mosque

Actually called the Jama Masjid this mosque was built in 1558 and gets its common name from its location in Kusumba, 42 km north of Rajshahi. It is pre-Moghul and considered one of the oldest in the region. The mosque is in traditional indigenous style, oblong in shape with six domes supported by pillars. There is also a ladies' gallery and three *mihrabs* carved with pilasters and adorned with arches in front, a peculiar characteristic of Muslim-Bangala architecture. It must have

Hindu Temple, Pabna

originated from the Buddhist practice of hollowing a part of the wall where a statue of the Buddha is usually placed for worship.

Getting There Buses depart for Kusumba from the bus station, near the railway station, in Rajshahi. The fare is Tk 11.

DACCA-RAJSHAHI
There are a couple of places of interest along the Dacca-Rajshahi route. Pabna on the road route, Natore on the rail route.

PABNA
This old town has a history that dates back to the medieval period. Some of the better specimens of pre-Moghul Bangala mosque architecture are to be found here. The Shahzadpur Mosque of 1528 is a single-domed mosque in traditional Bangala style. There are also some beautiful Hindu temples.

Places to Stay
Pabna hotels include the *Tripti Neloy* (tel 5290) at Radhanagar with rooms with attached bath for Tk 30-35 single, Tk 40-45 double. *Janata Boarding* on Abdul Hamid Rd has basic rooms for Tk 12/20. On the same road *Star Boarding* is similarly rock bottom in price and standards.

NATORE
This non-descript little town's main purpose is as a road junction. It is 152 km from Parbatipur, 65 km from Bogra and 44 km from Rajshahi. Its main claim to fame is that the president's second official residence, the Uttara Gana Bhavan, is located a few km to the north.

Places to Stay
The only hotel is the simple but clean *Natore Boarding* which charges Tk 12/25 for singles/doubles.

GAUR

Although none of the buildings from the Hindu kingdoms remain, Gaur is of great historical importance. There is only one mosque left, the Chotta Shona Masjid or 'Little Golden Mosque'. The rest has presumably been swallowed up by the jungle.

The Hindu Senas established their capital here and called it Lakhnauti. Just over a century later the Turkestan Khiljis took over and governed the region for more than three centuries until the Afghans replaced them. Under the Afghans Gaur became a prosperous city surrounded by fortified ramparts and a moat and spreading over 32 square km. Replete with temples, mosques and palaces the city was visited by traders and merchants from central Asia, Arabia, Persia and China.

Chotta Shona Masjid

Built in 1493-1526 this mosque originally had 15 gold domes and was built mainly of Rajmahal black stone. It had a ladies' gallery, arch gateways, ornately and lavishly decorated mihrabs and friezes depicting floral patterns on the walls. The stonework here is reputed to rival the havelis of Jaisalmer in Rajasthan in India. The nearby Bagha Mosque of 1523 is of similar design.

Other Mosques

The Rajbibi Mosque of 1490 and the Dorasbari Mosque of 1479 are of entirely different design to the Chotta Shona. The Shah Niamatullah Mosque of 1560 is in Firuzpur in Gaur. It has three domes and four squat towers.

Shah Shuja (1639-1660), the unfortunate eldest son of Shah Jahan and the Moghul viceroy of Bangala, built a palace in Rajmahal which he turned into his capital. It now stands right on the border, between the state of West Bengal in India and the Division of Rajshahi (near Gaur) in Bangladesh.

Getting There

Getting to Gaur takes a certain amount of logistical expertise: the route is via Nawabganj, 48 km north-west of Rajshahi. The minibus terminal in Rajshahi is a fair way from the town centre. The earliest minibuses depart at 6 am and the fare is Tk 10. At Nawabganj there is a ferry crossing of the Mahananda River which costs Tk 1.50 and takes 20 minutes to half an hour. You can hire the whole boat for Tk 6. Across the river you take a scooter microbus to Sipganj from where it is a further 48 km to Kanseth. Minibuses depart every two hours and the fare is Tk 7.

Finally it is 11 km from Kanseth to Gaur but the road, which has got steadily worse from Sipganj is now too rough for a motor vehicle, too rough in fact for a horse cart at anymore than a walking pace. It should cost Tk 70 for a horsecart to Gaur and back but the cost is likely to be twice that. Worse it's virtually impossible to get to Gaur and back in time for the last bus back to Sipganj at 3 pm. There is nowhere to stay apart from teashops in Kanseth while at the miserable teashops in Nawabganj even tea is likely to be *paowa jaina*!

Travel Reflections

The Mahananda River at Nawabganj is busy with all sorts of country watercraft from small paddle boats to the large flat-bottomed boats which transport buffalo and ox-carts across the river. On the road from Sipganj you can see buffalo-carts laden with fresh clay pots. Women tote them down to the river, the brittle-looking pots tied in a kind of net. Across the river menfolk carry pots of a different material – dull silvery aluminium.

In these rural parts of Bangladesh life is hard but gentle and tranquil although an obstructing buffalo cart can cause quite a stir. Still, it's a contrast to the urban bus drivers who deliberately halt their vehicles athwart the road, to stop following buses from getting ahead to pick up passengers further down the road.

Chittagong Division

Chittagong Division shares northern borders with the Indian states of Assam and Tripura, with Burma to the south-east, and Dacca Division along the Meghna River. The borderline with India and Burma runs through the forested hills of Assam, the Khastia and the Jayantia. These hills form the alpine region of what is essentially a very flat country; the average height of these hills is only 240 metres. Further south, in the Hill Tracts, the Pathua Hill chain maintains an average height of 650 metres. The highest peak in the country, Keokradong, 1320 metres, is to be found here.

The coastal strip from Chittagong is very narrow, crowded in to the sea by the hilly terrain to the east. This is the only coastal region of Bangladesh where the land is not fragmented by river deltas – in fact there is a long sandy beach stretching over 120 km to Teknaf, the most southerly town in the country.

There are five districts in the division: Sylhet in the north, Comilla below that, Noakhali in the south, and the two south-eastern districts, Chittagong and Chittagong Hill Tracts, adjacent to each other. The Mainimati region in the district of Comilla,

is considered the second most important archaeological site in the country. There are also been minor archaeological discoveries at Noakhali.

The history of the area is most notable for the Buddhist resistance against the invading Muslims who settled in and around Chittagong in the 12th century. Not until the latter part of the 17th century did the Moghuls extend their power this far and supersede the Buddhist Arakanese Kingdom of Burma in Chittagong. With the collapse of Moghul power it was the British who overran the various rulers although Portuguese pirates had long preyed upon the rich maritime trade of the region.

Of the four divisions in Bangladesh Chittagong is the second-most organized and developed in the country. It's population density is lower and the poverty less abject than in other parts of the country. Economically Sylhet District is known as the 'Land of Tea', while Chittagong District possesses the largest sea port.

CHITTAGONG DISTRICT
This is the hilliest district in the country,

and hence the region with the sparsest population. The hills are the dominant feature throughout, giving way to only one small section of plains at the base of the Pathua Hill chain. The beaches (or beach, as it's claimed to be the longest in the world) are long and broad. It commences at Sitakund and extends down to Patenga, where the estuary of the Karnapuli River cuts it off, then continues to Teknaf, just above the Burmese border.

Just off Cox's Bazar, the major southern town, are the islands of Sondwip, Hatia, and Kutubdia; further south are the Maheskhali and Sonadia islands, while just off Teknaf is the coral island of St Martin.

The word 'Chittagong' comes from the Arakanese phrase *Tsi-Tsi-Gong* inscribed on a tablet of these Buddhist invaders. It means 'That War Should Never Be Fought'. Chittagong appears to have been thriving as a port as early as Ptolemy's era (2nd century AD). He described it as one of the finest ports in the east. Later in the 9th century Arab merchants knew it as the seaport of Samunda and even took control of it for a short time.

Despite its name, Chittagong-the-city has been fought over in a fairly consistent fashion for the last four or five hundred years. In 1299 the Muslims occupied the city until the Arakanese re-took and retained it up to 1660. Then the Moghuls, in the process of extending their empire, took possession, only in turn to be expelled by the Arakanese in 1715. Prior to the arrival of the Moghuls the Dutch and the Portuguese had also figured prominently, but finally the British raised the flag in 1766. For the next one hundred years the Arakanese tried vainly to recapture the city, but only succeeded in aggravating the British sufficiently that in 1784 they pushed them back beyond the Naaf River, repelled them again in 1823 and finally, after another Arakanese onslaught in 1852, the British marched right in and took over Burma.

The two main racial types in this region are the Tibeto-Burmese Moghs and the Dravido-Aryans, the latter who have come to dominate in both number and religion. The Moghs have retreated to the hills in an attempt to maintain their religious and cultural identity. Despite Muslim control the atmosphere as you move south is quite different – quieter, gentler, more languid; more like Burma or Nepal than the subcontinent.

CHITTAGONG

Chittagong city, the second largest in Bangladesh, has a population of about one million. The climate is pleasant year round – it becomes cool in winter and only slightly humid in summer; annual rainfall is 2400 mm (twice Dacca's).

Located 264 km south-east of Dacca, the city takes its origins from trade and fishing. The port, the country's busiest, is on the western bank of the Karnapuli River. The city has the country's second international airport and is the jumping off point for the Chittagong Hill Tracts to the north and for Cox's Bazar further to the south.

It is also, in an old country, one of the oldest settlements, inhabited as early as the 2nd century AD. Xuan Zhang, the Chinese traveller, records the presence of the city in the 7th century as a 'sleeping beauty emerging out of the misty water.' The Mogh tribes were well established here when Portuguese traders razed it to the ground in 1538. Naming it Porto Grande it became the base of operations for the Portuguese traders who later went into brigandage. It was from here along with the island of Sondwip that they sallied out with their Mogh allies to prey on foreign vessels in the Bay of Bengal and on inland trading ports of the district of Dacca.

The evolution of the city followed a similar pattern to Dacca except that the oldest parts, located where Saddarghat now stands, were completely wiped out during the British and post-independence periods. When the British became masters

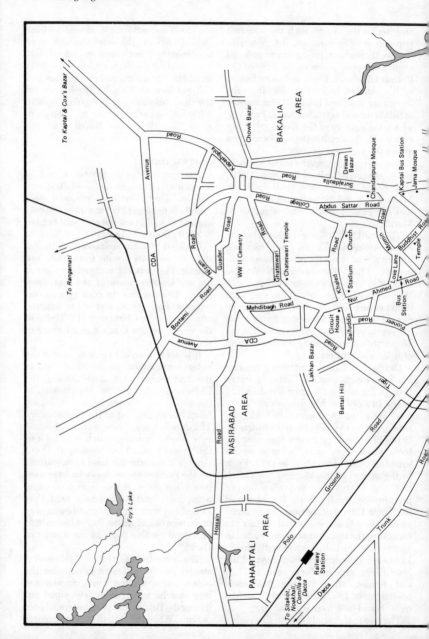

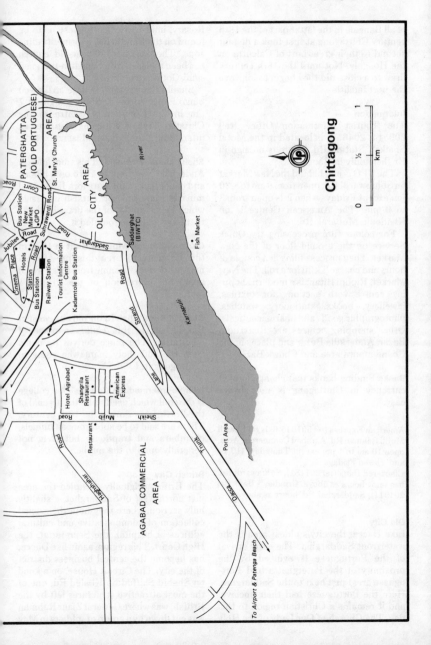

Chittagong

of all Bangala in the latter part of the 18th century Chittagong at first took a distant second to their great port of Calcutta on the Hooghly, Not until the 18th century drew to a close did they begin to improve the port facilities.

Information

The Tourist Information Office (tell 209514, 204650) is located in the Motel Shaikat, Station Rd. There is no sign in English, only in Bangala.

The GPO is just behind the New Market on Suhrawardi Rd; open from 8 am to 8.30 pm except Fridays when it is open from 3 to 9 pm. The American Centre is on Khadoum Mubarak Rd.

For colour film processing try Quick Service on the ground floor of the New Market. They process films in a couple of hours and charge Tk 30 for a roll. The New Market, Riponi Bitan, is a modern shopping centre with sections for textiles, jewellery, books, stationery, watches, photographic goods and pharmaceuticals. Other shopping centres are Reazzudin Bazar, Anderkilla Bazar and places in the Chandanpura area and Chowk Bazar.

Banks Finding banks that change foreign currency in Chittagong is not always easy.

American Express (tel 501045-6) is off Sheikh Mujib Rahman Rd, Agrabad Commercial Area, open 10 am to 1 pm except Thursdays (10-11 am), closed Fridays.
Chartered Bank (tel 201181), Suhrawardi Rd, has same hours as above. Grindlay's Bank (tel 201911), Saddarghat Rd, hours as above.

Old City

Like Dacca, the city's oldest area is the waterfront Saddarghat. The early arrival of the Portuguese is evinced by the proximity of the Paterghatta (old Portuguese area) just next to the Saddarghat. Here the Portuguese had their enclave, and it remains a Christian region to this day. The Church of Our Lady of the Holy Rosary, built by the Portuguese, is to be found on the Bandle Rd, a former trading zone. The original 350-year-old church has been replaced by a Canadian-designed semi-Gothic structure.

Should the irresistible urge strike you bingo is played every Sunday night at 7 pm in the Community Centre in the Christian area. Chittagong also has an interesting Ethnological Museum.

Shahi Jama-e-Masjid This mosque in Anderkilla, was built in 1670 on a hillock and hence looks a bit like a fort. It has a tall minaret, Saracenic or Turkish in design which looms up out of the press of shops that have since surrounded it.

Qadam Mubarak Mosque Built in 1336 in the Rahmatganj area this pre-Moghul mosque derives its name from a slab which bears an impression of the Prophet's foot.

Chilla of Badar Shah In the old city, west of Bakshirhat, is this *chilla* or place of meditation. The place derives its name from the sufi (holy man) who came to Chittagong in 1336.

Islamic Intermediate College This college is on a hill which used to be the arsenal of the Portuguese during the 16th century. There are said to be subterranean tunnels, chambers and trapdoors but it is not generally open to the public.

British City

The British originally occupied the area just north-west of Saddarghat, a slightly hilly section, where they built their usual collection of administrative and cultural edifices; a hospital, the Secretariat, the High Court. This region, again like Dacca, has become the central business district of the city. The Circuit House, on a knoll on Shahid Saiffuddin Khaled Rd, one of the most attractive structures left by the British, was where General Ziaur Rahman was cut down by a group of soldiers in May

1980. The British area retains its colonial air and comparative sense of order and cleanliness.

Chandanpura Mosque On the street of the same name this mosque is north of the centre on the road to Kaptai. It has no historical importance but is an attractive sight due to its delicate design.

High Court Building On Fairy Hill there is a panoramic view of Karnapuli and the city from this British building.

Modern City

In the post-war period, Chittagong was still primarily made up of mud dwellings divided by wide dusty streets. The appearance of concrete and more modern materials is a reflection of the city's new found status as premier port and second city. The Agrabad Commercial Area with its banks, large hotels and corporate offices is quite in keeping with the trends of a 20th-century city. Along with this has come all the problems of such a life as applied to Bangladesh; a maelstrom of rickshaws, innumerable beggars and roads potholed beyond belief. The outer reaches of the city have become industrialized; the only steel mill and oil refinery in Bangladesh are located in Chittagong. Many other smaller industries producing cigarettes, matches and plywood are based here as well.

World War II Cemetery Though perhaps not on everybody's list of must-see's, this cemetery contains the graves of soldiers from both the Allied and Japanese sides who died fighting on the Burma front. It is well maintained and located on Fazul Rd.

Chittagong Port

The port of Chittagong is located on the west bank of the Karnapuli River, 15 km from its confluence with the Kapurtali River. Ocean-going vessels have to be guided up the river by local pilots from the Patenga lighthouse. There are three sandbars to be crossed – the Outer Bar, Inner Bar and Gupta Bar with depths varying from seven to 10 metres depending on the tides. Chittagong now has 20 berths and handles bulk cargoes and container ships – up to 900 vessels and 5.5 million tons annually. The port has made Chittagong the commercial centre of Bangladesh as well as the second largest and second most important city in the country. Unfortunately the rail, road and river transportation facilities from Chittagong are barely able to cope with the port's cargo handling facilities.

Places to Stay – bottom end

With the exception of five-star hotels all the hotels in Chittagong are better value than those of Dacca.

The *United Hotel*, 128 Golapsing Lane, is just off Jubilee Rd, a short distance from the Safina. It's a quiet place with rooms with shared baths at Tk 20/30. *Hotel Chittagong*, Sheikh Mujib Rahman Rd in the Agrabad Commercial Area, has the same rates and standard as the United.

The *Imperial Hotel*, Royal Rd, is a fairly old building but has a friendly atmosphere. Rooms with shared bath are Tk 13/20 for singles/doubles. The *Eastern Hotel* on K C Day Rd is a run down old establishment which has seen better days.

The *YMCA* at 150 Jubilee Rd is normally for local students staying on a monthly basis, but has a room reserved for foreign tourists: dorm bed Tk 25, the whole room Tk 30. The *Tourist Hotel*, Jubilee Rd, near the Cox's Bazar bus terminal is entered via a passageway through a sweetshop. The sign is only in Bangala so you will have to ask. Rooms on the street side are good value at Tk 15/25 but beware of bed bugs.

Places to Stay – middle

Hotel Dream International on Station Rd is fairly new and has a rather unreliable restaurant. Rooms are Tk 55-60 single,

Tk 80-90 double. *Hotel Miskha* (tel 203623), Station Rd, is one of those old, quiet establishments with the remnants of a British Raj atmosphere. There's a restaurant and singles/doubles are Tk 45/75.

Hotel Safina (tel 201442) at 50 Jubilee Rd is an old fashioned place with rooms with both shared and attached baths. Overall it is not very clean, particularly the bed linen. Rooms are Tk 32/50 or Tk 40/75 with bath. The 4th floor restaurant does a pseudo-western breakfast for Tk 12 or meals for Tk 30-40 – your money is better spent in a Chinese restaurant.

Hotel Manila, Station Rd, is newish, clean, has a small dining hall and is usually full. All rooms have attached bath and singles/doubles are Tk 40/65. *Hotel Al-Amin*, in the bazar behind Hotel Safina, is in a new but rapidly decaying building. Despite which it is kept running fairly well and rooms with shared bath are good value at Tk 20/35. *Hotel Raj*, 154 Kabi Nazral Islam Savah, Saddarghat, is a huge place, with many rooms at Tk 80/120 for singles/doubles. And, reported a traveller, 'heaps of employees falling over themselves to help you'.

Places to Stay – top end

Hotel Agrabad (tel 500111-20), Agrabad Commercial Area, is the classiest in town with appropriate rates that range from Tk 675 to Tk 1656. Facilities include the usual amenities (bar, swimming pool, roof garden, shopping arcade and so on).

Motel Shaikat (tel 204650-209845), Station Rd, is run by Parjatan and the Tourist Information Office is located here. There are only double rooms with rates Tk 300-390. It has a fairly good restaurant, and is located right across from the Hotel Miskha.

Hotel Shahjahan (tel 208660), Saddarghat Rd, is very new with singles, doubles, suites from Tk 115 to 200. It has a restaurant, bar and bank. *Hotel Hawaii* (tel 504057), 39 Agrabad Commercial Area is pretty modern with phones,

restaurant, bar and a bank for foreign currencies. Rates are from Tk 97 to 150.

Places to Eat

Like Dacca there are a fair number of Chinese restaurants, most of them locally run. Most local eating places in Chittagong are better value than Dacca.

Cheaper *Cafe Ferdous* on Station Rd has good food. *New Market Restaurant*, first floor at the corner of Jubilee Rd and Suhrawardi Rd, has a fairly good local menu. *Cafe Iran & Restaurant*, to the left of the Hotel Safina on Jubilee Rd, is good value for local dishes.

The *Gulistan Restaurant* on Suhrawardi Rd mainly does chicken curry and rice for around Tk 12. The *Railway Station Restaurant* has simple local fare but it's cheap and clean with meals at Tk 12-16. Eating places in the bazar near the Hotel Al-Amin are good value, especially for the popular 'Chittagong Beef'.

Jubilee Rd is the best place to find an eating house to suit your needs. Even the cheap ones are pretty good by comparison with the rest of the country.

More Expensive *Chungking Restaurant*, Sheikh Mujib Rahman Rd, Agrabad Commercial Area, opposite Dewan Hat, is one of the oldest Chinese establishments and is reputed to have the best cuisine in town. Prices are the same as other Chinese restaurants and smaller quantity is compensated by excellent quality. On the other hand the *Shangrila Chinese Restaurant*, 39 Agrabad Commercial Area, off Sheikh Mujib Rahman Rd, serves very large quantities although they occasionally have no ice cream or coffee.

The *Shanghai Chinese Restaurant* is opposite Funkinhat on Airport Rd. The *Gate of London Chinese Restaurant* is on Saiffuddin Khaled Rd. The *Hongkong Restaurant & Bar* is on Strand Rd in the port area. The *Chin Lung Restaurant* is on Suhrawardi Rd below Fairy Hill. On Jubilee Rd at the corner with Love Lane, five minutes walk west from the Hotel Safina, is the *Tai Wah Restaurant*. Two others are the *Tung Fung Chinese Restaurant* and the *Toh Ka Lin Chinese Restaurant*, both on K B Fazul Qader Rd.

Chinese restaurants in town are only open from 11 am till 3 pm and again from 6 to 10.30 pm.

Entertainment

There is hardly any entertainment in Chittagong except in top-end hotels like Hotel Agrabad where they have a disco on Friday and Saturday nights.

Liquor is easily available except that foreign brand whiskey is extremely expensive. Many restaurants have bars although generally only for local brand drinks.

Getting There & Away

Chittagong has air, rail and road links with Dacca; ferry links with Barisal; air links with Calcutta and Jessore; air, launch and road links with Cox's Bazar; and rail and road links with Comilla and Sylhet.

Air There are three flights daily with Biman between Chittagong and Dacca, the fare is Tk 450. To Cox's Bazar there are four flights a week at a fare of Tk 145 and in summer this flight can be booked out weeks ahead. Check with the Biman office for the latest news on the Jessore flight. There's one flight a week to Calcutta with a fare of Tk 1093.

Airline offices in Chittagong are:

Bangladesh Biman (tel 206081-5), Jasmine Palace, Nur Ahmed Sarak Rd.
Air India (tel 504767), Hotel Agrabad.
Indian Airlines (tel 838542), Hotel Agrabad.
Pakistan International Airline (tel 502908), Hotel Agrabad.

There isn't always a bus to meet incoming flights at Chittagong, the airport is a long way out from town and autorickshaws tend to be very expensive. If you walk out of the airport a half km to the the T-junction you can catch a local bus right into the New Market.

River To Barisal the BIWTC ferry operates twice a week on Monday and Thursday, takes 24 hours and costs Tk 284 in 1st class, Tk 189 in 2nd, Tk 85 in Interclass, Tk 57 in deck class. Usually 1st and 2nd-class cabins are booked weeks in advance. The route is via Sondwip and Hatia.

To Cox's Bazar there's a BIWTC seatruck twice a week. It takes two days and the fare is Tk 14. There is a stop midway at Kutubdia for a whole day. A tough but interesting trip.

There are private launches to outlying coastal areas and islands off the coast. If you're in an exploring mood check the launch trips at Saddarghat.

Rail Four to six trains daily leave Dacca for Chittagong; two are mail or express trains, two are ordinary. It is an eight to 10-hour trip; 1st class Tk 203, 2nd class Tk 55, 3rd class Tk 24. The trains include the Ulka Express, Karnapuli Express, Janta Mail and the Dacca Mail Express.

To Sylhet, via Comilla, there's only one direct train daily, the morning Chittagong Express. The trip takes 12 hours and fares are Tk 230 in 1st, Tk 60 in 2nd, Tk 27 in 3rd.

To Comilla takes four to six hours at a cost of Tk 102 in 1st, Tk 26 in 2nd, Tk 11 in 3rd. Noakhali trains go via Laksham and also to Chandpur. There are four connecting trains daily and the fare for the 1½ to two hour trip is Tk 30.50 in 2nd, Tk 13.50 in 3rd.

Road From Dacca buses for Chittagong presently go from the Eastern Gate, near Gulistan Bazar. The trip takes eight to 10 hours and involves two ferry crossings. A night express bus (complete with TV) costs Tk 55 and departs at 8.30 pm. Day express buses cost Tk 42 to 46.

For buses from Chittagong there is not, as of yet, any central bus terminal. Bus stations are scattered around the city centre. Details are as follow:

New Market This is the station for BRTC buses for Dacca (Tk 42) and Cox's Bazar (Tk 22) from 9 am to 1 pm.

Jubilee Rd This station is right in front of the Hotel Safina and has private buses for Dacca and Cox's Bazar from 6 am to 3 pm. Day express buses to Dacca cost Tk 45, night expresses Tk 55. The trip takes six to eight hours. For Cox's Bazar departures are from 8.30 am and the four hour trip costs Tk 26. The express bus at 9 am only takes 3½ hours and costs Tk 28.

Cinema Place This is a terminal for Cox's Bazar, Rangamati and other outlying areas. Buses depart from 6 am to 3 pm. To Cox's Bazar it's mainly express minibuses and the fare is Tk 32. To Rangamati the buses take 2½ hours and cost Tk 12.

Love Lane This terminal is a departure point for Dacca buses from 6 am to 3 pm. Night express buses also go from here.

Kadam Tole Buses depart from here from 6 am to 3 pm for Comilla, Dacca, Sitakund and Noakhali. The aircon day buses to Dacca also go from here – fares are Tk 80 to 105.

Madibari This is the terminal for buses for Sitakund, Noakhali, Feni, Laksham and Comilla. Sitakund buses take 30 minutes to an hour and cost Tk 4-5. Comilla buses take 3½ hours and cost Tk 18.

Anderkilla This is the bus station for Kaptai with departures from 6 am to 3 pm. The fare for the 1½ hour trip is Tk 7.

Getting Around

There are very few taxis and autorickshaws in Chittagong. Generally urban transport is by rickshaw, with fares very similar to Dacca.

Airport Transport The airport is in the Patenga area, about 16 km south of the city. There is no public transport, so a taxi fare of Tk 60-80 or babytaxi fare of Tk 30-40 is to be expected. Make certain the fare is absolutely agreed on before departing!

If you want to get a bus you can walk out from the airport buildings to a T-intersection and take the local bus which goes to New Market. There is apparently a Biman staff bus that leaves for the airport before flight time, so it might be worth checking with Biman about this to scrounge a lift.

AROUND CHITTAGONG
Mazhar of Sultan Bayazid Bostami

This hilltop shrine is in the Wazirabad area, seven km north-west of the city. At the foot of the hill is a pond full of turtles which legend says were the descendants of evil spirits, turned into turtles by the curse of a saint over a thousand years ago. A great *mela* (festival) is held here during the Muslim festival of Shab-e-Bharat.

Pahartali Lake

Further beyond the Bostami Mazhar this lake is a used as a picnic spot and has boating facilities. It's easier to get to by train rather than bus.

Shatpura

This small village, 24 km south of the city, has Buddhist and Hindu temples. The Nindam Kanon Temple here is a meditation centre. There's no public transport in this direction so it can be difficult to get to.

Patenga Beach

There is also no public transport to this deserted beach, 24 km south of the city via the airport road. Taxis should cost Tk 60 to 80, babytaxis Tk 30 to 40, but they usually jack up their fares because of the difficulty of finding a passenger for the return trip.

Fouzdharat Beach

For similar reasons of difficulty with transport this beach, 16 km south of Chittagong, is equally deserted.

DACCA-CHITTAGONG

The road from Dacca to Comilla is one of the better highways in Bangladesh. About two hours out there's a ferry crossing of the Meghna before Comilla. Buses tend to wait for a long time at Comilla. So long that the trains, which make a long loop up to Bhairab Bazar before descending down to Comilla via Akhaura Junction, are just as fast. Trains do have the advantage of a bridge over the Meghna, whereas buses usually have a half hour or so wait for the ferry and then the crossing can take another half hour.

From Comilla the road and railway run almost parallel to Chittagong. The bus makes a quick stop in Feni then continues past Sitakund and soon after runs along the coast to Chittagong.

FENI

This pleasant little town is a road junction to Comilla, Noakhali and Chittagong.

Places to Stay

The best place to stay is the *Hotel Dinofa* on College Rd, Tk 20 for a double with shared bath, Tk 12 for a single.

Getting There

There are direct buses from here to Noakhali but no direct bus line to Chandpur.

SITAKUND

This sleepy little town, 36 km to the west of Chittagong, is on the Dacca-Chittagong road and rail lines. Sitakund itself is not the purpose of any visit, but rather the Hindu Chandranath temples located six km away. Unless you have a particular interest in Hindu temples the only time it's really worth a visit is during the Shiva-Chaturdashi Festival, held here for 10 days in February. It's an hour's hard climb to the hill top temple. Sitakund's Buddhist temple is just a ramshackle wooden building, not worth the effort.

Getting There

Take a bus for Noakhali from the Kadam Tole bus station in Chittagong, the trip takes 45 minutes and costs Tk 4-6.

LAKSHAM

A quiet small town boasting only a busy railway junction for Comilla, Noakhali, Chandpur and Chittagong.

Getting There

The Dacca-Chittagong and the Chittagong-Sylhet (via Comilla) trains stop here for passengers making a connection with Noakhali and Chandpur trains. This is the best connection for Chandpur if coming from either Comilla or Chittagong.

NOAKHALI

This was the site of much bloodshed between Hindus and Muslims at the time of partition. Mahatma Ghandi visited this place to pacify the rioting communities.

There are negligible remains of the ancient Buddhist settlements visited by Xuan Zhang in the 7th century. Don't expect too much but it could be an interesting diversion en route to Chandpur by launch. The Bajra Shahi Mosque of 1741 has fine paintings of floral design.

CHITTAGONG HILL TRACTS DISTRICT

Its lush tropical vegetation and unique concentration of tribal cultures has made this district the central tourist region in Bangladesh. Covering 8200 square km and with a population of just over one million, it is ideally suited both environmentally and climatically to tourism.

It is ironic, however, that it is also the most troubled region in the whole country and for this reason has become a restricted area. Foreigners are permitted only to visit Rangamati and Kaptai; access to the hinterland is rarely permitted.

The troubles stem from the culture clash between the varied tribal peoples who are the original inhabitants of this region, and the plains people who have begun to develop this region, both physically and for its potential to attract tourists.

The construction of the Kaptai Lake for hydro-electricity in the 1960s submerged 40% of the land used by the tribes for cultivation and displaced 100,000 people. The land provided for resettlement was not sufficient and many tribes fled into neighbouring Indian Assam and Tripura. The problem was further compounded by the plains people using traditional tribal lands for their own cultivation.

In the 1970s, the tribes, led by the Chakmas, united to form the *Shanti Bahini*, Peace Army, with the aim of protecting their culture, language and way of life, and to strive for political autonomy. Inter-tribal rivalry shattered the union, leaving the problem to simmer until 1978 when 200,000 ethnic Indian Muslims were expelled from Burma. These refugees ended up in the Chittagong Hill Tracts where they began to establish colonies in the Matranga region. The tribes, once again feeling threatened by the encroachment of foreigners, attacked and destroyed several of the new settlers' villages. As a consequence, the district was put under military administration which has only added to the resentment of the tribespeople. Many tribes have moved across the border into India, creating a point of irritation in Indo-Bangladeshi relations.

On top of all these problems, oil was discovered in parts of the Hill Tracts, increasing disruption for the tribes. The outlawing of the Shanti Bahini as a political party led its members to begin guerrilla-style operations against the authorities. In January 1984 they abducted five foreign members of an oil exploration team in protest against the government's failure to solve their problems. The foreigners were later released. Some good seems to have come of this, with the government offering a general amnesty to the guerrillas, and the commencement of talks with tribal leaders.

Restricted Areas

Though all regions in the Hill Tracts are restricted areas for foreigners except for Rangamati and Kaptai, the following regions are mentioned should there be any change in official attitudes.

Gumara, an area rich in wildlife including tigers, deer and birdlife; Manikcheri, the capital of the Maung tribe; Pangarh, accessible by paved road; Barkal, a scenic spot in the Lushai Hills; the Kassalong and Sajek valleys inhabited by the Lushai tribe, once headhunters but now Christian converts and amongst the most developed of the ethnic groups; Mainimukh, a little island on the lake north-east of Rangamati; Ramgarh and Kragacheri, idyllic spots surrounded by dense forest. All these at the time of publication *were* off-limits, but things are always changing . . . .

Trekking Permits

Officially you must apply in Dacca to the Wildlife Section of the Forestry Department, then visit Army Headquarters for a permit, then the Ministry of Home Affairs. Application forms are handed over *pro forma* which must then be submitted to your consulate or embassy. The intention seems to be to have you register with your consular officials when visiting a disturbed area. Processing supposedly takes about a week but actually you're unlikely to ever hear anymore about it! Permits are virtually impossible to obtain.

RANGAMATI

Rangamati is built on a small ismuth on the shores of Lake Kaptai and joined to the mainland by a small causeway. The countryside is lush, undulating and verdant. There is a police checkpost on the outskirts of the town where you must complete a Foreigner's Registration form which takes about three-quarters of an hour to process and receive the desired permit.

The region is still politically volatile, so take heed of the sensibilities of the local authorities.

Information

Don't bother visiting the Tourist Information Office (tel 366, 236) which is inconveniently located at the Tourist Motel on Deer Hill. They know little if anything at all about tourism. Of course this may have changed but meanwhile it's better to save your taxi fare and ask somebody first.

Tribal woven fabrics from Rangamati are of excellent quality with simple but beautiful patterns. The Sonargaon Hotel in Dacca occasionally holds a fair for local handicrafts and textiles.

Things to See & Do
This is a good place to take a breather away from some of the more debilitating aspects of travel in Bangladesh. Walking, swimming, boating, sunbathing and exploring the uninhabited small islands just off the peninsulas are the main forms of amusements.

The Buddhist water festival, held 13-18 April each year, is a colourful event.

Eight km to the north is the island of Ranga Pani where the Raj Bana Vihara, the Kings's Forest Temple, is located. Five km further is the rajbari or royal area. Twenty km to the north is the Long Gordu Meditation Centre, located in a forest reserve. Across the lake, eight km from the rajbari and visible from there on top of a mountain, is the Jawnasouk Mountain Vihara. Unfortunately it's in the restricted area.

The outlying areas are the tribal lands of the Chakma tribe, but whether you can visit is dependent on the political situation.

A permit is required if you wish to travel on the lake.

Places to Stay & Eat
Hotel *Wilderness* (tel 205) is in the Kattoltole area and has rooms with bath for Tk 60 but is poor value. *De Rangamati Boarding*, near the museum, is an old building with singles at Tk 40 and doubles for Tk 60. The *Al Mahmud Hotel*, just a short distance away from the bus station, has singles/doubles with shared bath for Tk 15/25. There's a nice verandah overlooking the lake and the fellow in charge can prepare some food. The *Gulistan Hotel* is good value at Tk 12/20.

The *Boarding House* is right on Tobolchuri Ghat and offers basic accommodation for Tk 10-15 a room; it's actually a traveller's inn and foreign tourists have to bargain a bit. *Hotel Hiramund*, opposite the New Court Building, has been recommended with rooms at Tk 30/50. They also have good food and it's a Tk 1 ride from the bazars.

The *Tourist Motel* (tel 236, 366) on Deer Hill has a restaurant, bar and boat-hire. Double rooms are Tk 180 or Tk 300 with aircon. The *Tourist Cottages* is at the bottom of Deer Hill near the boat-hire. Each cottage unit has a kitchen for those who wish to do their own cooking. The rate for an eight-bed cottage is Tk 390, for four-bed Tk 270. It is apparently not open to individual travellers, you have to rent a whole cottage.

Getting There
River BIWTC ferries from Barisal go to Rangamati then back to Chittagong.

Road It's 70 km from Chittagong to Rangamati. The bus departs from the Cinema Place depot in Chittagong and the trip takes 2½ hours, including the delay at the police check point. The fare is Tk 12. If you're intending to visit Kaptai as well as Rangamati you can go to either town first but it makes more sense to go to Rangamati then Kaptai. The bus is usually very crowded when it departs Chittagong so get on early. On the way you pass a satellite tracking station at Betbunia.

On arrival in Rangamati you have to get off the bus to register at the Special Branch Police Station's Foreigner's Registration section. Take your pack with you as the whole process takes 45 minutes and the buses do not wait for foreigners while they obtain the necessary permit. Rangamati-Chittagong buses are also very crowded so reserve a seat or get on early if you don't want to stand the whole way.

Getting Around

A babytaxi from the police station to the tourist office in the Tourist Motel on Deer Hill should cost Tk 3-5 although they will stridently demand Tk 20 upon arrival! It's about a two km distance, all uphill. You can hire canoes on the lake from Tk 10 per hour, or speedboats for Tk 275 per hour.

LAKE TRIP

There are innumerable launch trips one can make on this artificial 426-square-km lake but a special lake permit is required. Whether your permit is in line with the rules governing restricted access in this area is up to the little man who vets your destination ticket as you embark. It's worth finding out exactly where each launch is going and how long it takes; if you get caught out overnight, hotel proprietors have been known to report overdue tourists 'missing', causing problems with the authorities. Travellers have managed to get to Mainimukh, supposedly forbidden to foreigners, simply by getting on the wrong boat!

A permitted trip is to Kaptai, which some people consider a must while in Bangladesh. There are two launches a day which leave at 8.30 am and at 3.30 pm from the end of the Reserve Bazar. The launch does not always go from the Boat Club near the Tourist Cottages, sometimes it only departs from Tobolchuri Ghat so it is wise to be there half an hour or so before departure time. Make sure you're on the right boat too. There are a number of services operating on the lake and it's easy to end up at the wrong place.

If you get the launch with the rooftop, sit there as it gets cramped underneath, but keep any camera out of sight as the military are very much in evidence and very sensitive. There are a couple of army checkpoints where the cargo is scrutinised along the way. The trip takes about 1½ hours and cost about Tk 7. There is no need to backtrack to Rangamati as you can continue from Kaptai to Chittagong.

KAPTAI

Kaptai is the site for a spillway and administrative offices for the hydro-electricity project, so it's not set up for tourists to the extent of Rangamati. There is not a great deal to do here, and the atmosphere is rather oppressive: no photography or unauthorised movement. The Kaptai ghat looks quite picturesque at night, though.

It is a flat town with one main street consisting of a long row of low structures; this is the bazar where all the eating places, hotels and boarding houses, tea-shops and general stores are located. There is one two-storey building. Kaptai's main source of development comes from the 80 megawatt hydro-electric project nearby. Fears for its safety contribute to the rather over-the-top security measures in the region.

Places to Stay & Eat

There is no tourist office. The *Government Rest House* apparently requires prior permission to use. The two-storey structure is the *Kamal Boarding House* which graciously accepts tourists. It is reasonably clean with common bathing facilities; singles/doubles are Tk 25/45. There are also cheapies here which are pretty basic, like the *Sat Khana Boarding House* which offers a dorm bed for Tk 5, a single for Tk 7.

Although the menu at Kaptai's few eating places tends to be limited to rice and chicken curry the food is good – the rice is fresh and steaming, not the usual stale leftovers. Breakfast – parathas, halva and tea – is pretty good too.

Getting There

Kaptai is 58 km from Chittagong. Buses leave from just at the end of Anderkilla Rd near the American Cultural Centre and the trip takes 1½ hours. A turnoff towards the Karnapuli River, 22 km from Chittagong, leads to the village of Batagi, seven km off the road. This is reportedly a pleasant area for short hikes. It's better to

Top: Bedyas, the river-gypsies of Bangladesh (GW)
Left: Bedyas encampment (GW)
Right: Hindu fisherman at Heron Point on the edge of the Bay of Bengal, Khulna Division (GW)

Top: bazar on Jubilee Rd, Chittagong (JRS)
Bottom: laying out fishing nets, Cox's Bazar, Chittagong Division (JRS)

make the loop from Chittagong in the direction Chittagong-Rangamati-Kaptai.

CHITMORONG

This is a Buddhist village of the Marmas tribe, five km from Kaptai on the road to Chandraghona, 26 km further south. The bus will drop you off at a bus stop with a milestone; there is no village in sight but the rooftop of the pagoda-like monastery can be seen above the trees. There is a footpath on the left which ends at the top of a rather steep concrete stairway; at the bottom, you hope, waits a boat to ferry you across to the village for about Tk 1.

Part of the attraction of Chitmorong is the languid, serene atmosphere. Amongst the bamboo and thatched village huts you can purchase a cup of the local palm wine, *tari*. The village contains some richly adorned Buddhist sculptures and the monastery is presided over by an English-speaking head monk. On the hilltop is a huge stupa with a temple to one side. Here you may come across the head monk, who will chat with you over a cup of tea (your donation). A Buddhist festival is held here every Bengali New Year, around mid-April.

Getting There There is a military checkpoint before Chitmorong but buses seldom stop or get checked here. By bus it's only Tk 0.75; by babytaxi Tk 10-15 depending on your powers of persuasion.

BANDARBAN

Bandarban, south-east of Chittagong and south of Kaptai, is the administrative centre of the district, a military cantonment and hence a restricted area. This, however, is not necessarily so as the town does not appear within the restricted zone and is, moreover, linked by road to Kaptai in the north and Satkania in the south via the Chittagong-Cox's Bazar road. This is worth checking out.

Places to Stay
The *Hotel Tripti* in Bandarban Bazar has

rooms with common bath for Tk 12/24. *Carwar Boarding* in the town centre is similarly priced.

CHANDRAGHONA

This industrial centre has Asia's biggest paper mill as well as a rayon production complex and jute mills. Unless you're very interested in local industrial development there is nothing to see. You are supposed to surrender your permit from Kaptai at the police checkpost before Chitmorong but buses do not stop there.

COX'S BAZAR DISTRICT

This district, adjacent to the Chittagong Hill Tracts, runs south down the coastline to the Burmese border. It has an area of 1300 square km and a population of about one million who are a mix of Muslims, Hindus and Buddhists of Arakanese descent. It is the meeting point of Indo-Burmese races, languages and cultures. The culture here is less overtly Muslim, or even Hindu for that matter, having a more Burmese-Buddhist atmosphere.

This region was a favourite of the Mogh pirates and brigands who with the Portuguese used to ravage the Bay of Bengal in the 17th century. The Moghs have remained, maintaining their tribal ways through handicrafts and cottage industries such as the manufacture of cheroots and handwoven fabrics. To some degree the Moghs have assimilated more than other tribes into the ways of the dominant Muslim culture.

In the middle of the 17th century Shah Shuja, son of Shah Jahan, elder brother of Aurangzeb and viceroy of Bangala for 17 years (1643-1660) went to the rescue of his father who had been imprisoned by Aurangzeb. The rescue attempt failed and he had to flee for his life but back in Dacca he found no help and was forced to continue further east to the region of the Arakan Kingdom of Burma.

He passed through Cox's Bazar, apparently with a thousand palanquins although only 40 of the one-thousand-strong harem accompanied him. He encamped at what is now known as Dulahazara, now a village north-west of Cox's Bazar – the name comes from Hazrat Doli, 'One Thousand Palanquins'. In the Arakanese kingdom he was welcomed at first but Moghul intrigue made the Arakanese king decide to dispatch him and his entire retinue in 1660.

When Moghul power declined the region came briefly under the Portuguese and their Mogh allies who in turn were driven out by the British. Cox's Bazar fell to the British in 1760 and the town was founded by Captain Hiram Cox with a Roang Mogh colony, presumably to protect it against the Burmese.

COX'S BAZAR

The town of Cox's Bazar, 152 km south-east of Chittagong, is the administrative centre of the district. It derives its name from Captain Hiram Cox who in 1798 was commissioned to settle the region with Arakanese immigrants from Burma. Primarily known for its long, shark-free beaches (though a few jellyfish), Cox's Bazar has become a central tourist resort. It gets booked up in the winter holiday season but crowds still tend to gather at the first sign of western tourists.

The town is set on rolling hills, and due to its foreign appeal has a considerable number of foreign buildings, mostly hotels. The town is divided into enclaves, one for the Moghs and the other for Bangalas with the latter tending to dominate in number.

The colourful Buddhist Water Festival takes place from 13 to 18 April each year.

Information

The Uttara Bank, located at the Sayeman Hotel, accepts foreign currencies and cashes travellers' cheques. The Tourist Information Office appears to have moved from the Motel Upal to the nearby Hotel Shaibal. There is no tour service, but they have jeeps and minibuses for hire.

The Handicraft Emporium at Karpupannya Cottage Industries, Motel Rd, has a variety of excellent quality handicrafts: jute products, mainly doormats, carpets, wall-hangings. The leatherwork is mainly purses and handbags and they also have woodwork and ceramic items plus handwoven fabrics, silk and cotton. There are other handicraft shops including Burmese shops near the Buddhist monastery in town. Here you will find handwoven fabrics, saris, longhis and jewellery.

Police noticeboards at the beach warn you not to stay in isolated places without informing the police, not to get too for out in the water (there are no lifeguards) and that swimming at low tide is risky. The police beach post can advise on the best times and places to swim. Non-residents can use the pool at the Sayeman Hotel for Tk 10.

Things to See & Do

Apart from the minor attractions of a Buddhist monastery, the launch ghat and the fish market, Cox's Bazar is principally a beach resort, and Saikat is the main beach. Motel Rd leads to this beach which has a few kiosks and souvenir shops, mostly with seashell crafts. The beach is very broad and stretches endlessly to the north and south. The locals tend to swim fully clothed, so if you're inclined to do with less than this, walk 15-20 minutes away from the Seabeach Rd end or be prepared for a very large audience.

The most interesting places to see, besides the beaches, are to be found on day or overnight trips along the coast and into the countryside. Unless, of course, you're just interested in getting a tan.

Places to Stay – bottom end

Al-Belal Boarding on Sea Beach Rd is basic with shared bath singles/doubles at Tk 15/25. There are other cheapies on a lane which cuts southward from the bus station towards the launch ghat. Some are being renovated and are likely to have their rates pushed up when completed.

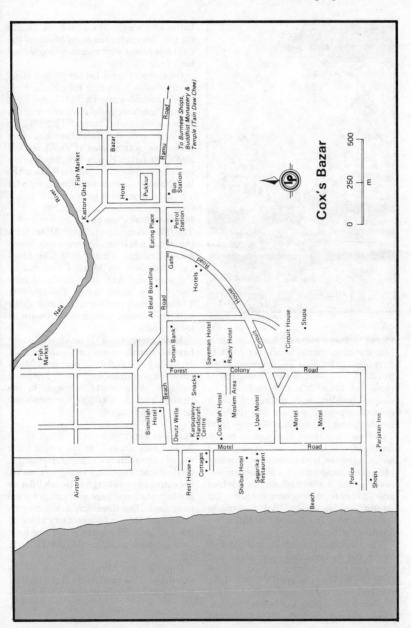

Cox's Bazar

Buddhist Temple, Cox's Bazar

Places to Stay – middle

Non-Parjatan tourist hotels tend not to have signs in English. The *Sayeman Hotel* (tel 231) on Forest Colony Rd is in the centre of town. It's a three-storey U-shaped building with restaurant and a swimming pool. There are only doubles, family rooms and suites with rates from Tk 70 to 165. *Hotel Rachy*, next to the Sayeman, looks like a British-period boarding house. It's a cleanish place with a pleasant atmosphere (if a bit noisy in the evening) and shared bath singles/doubles are Tk 20/40. Foreigners get 10% off during the high season, 25% discount in the off-season. The *Tourist Rest House* has doubles for Tk 50.

The *Bismillah Hotel & Restaurant*, Sea Beach Rd, is basic but fairly clean and quiet and the restaurant is good. Shared bath singles/doubles are Tk 20/40. Like the Rachy the *Hotel Cox Wah* on Motel Rd is always full during the holiday season. There are rooms with shared and attached

baths with singles/doubles from Tk 25/60. On Cinema Rd the *Hotel Mermaid* (tel 633) has rooms with common or attached bath from Tk 25 to 50.

On Circuit House Rd the *Niribili Hotel* is good value but often fully booked up. Singles/doubles are Tk 25/35. Adjacent to the Niribili the *Hotel Kohinoor* only has rooms with shared bath at Tk 20/35. In the same area the *Hotel Fanoa* is more expensive, with singles at Tk 55-60, but also quite basic. Finally the *Parjatan Inn* is at the extreme end of Motel Rd near the beach and has rooms with shared bath for Tk 25/50 plus dorm beds at Tk 20.

Places to Stay – top end

The *Hotel Shaibal* (tel 275) on Motel Rd is the classiest in town. There are only aircon doubles costing Tk 300-600. The *Motel Upal* (tel 258) on Motel Rd is run by Parjatan and has only aircon double rooms with rates from Tk 200-300. There's a bar, restaurant, tourist shops and the tourist information centre is located here.

Motel Probal (tel 211) on Motel Rd also has only double rooms for Tk 150 and up. *Motel Labonee* (tel 403) is also on Motel Rd and has doubles for Tk 100. There are cottages along Motel Rd built in the British period, Tk 300 for two-room units.

Places to Eat

Remarkably enough, at last count there was not one solitary Chinese restaurant in Cox's Bazar. For cheap eating you can try the eating places along Sea Beach Rd near the bus station – here you can get good local food. The *Bismillah Restaurant* on Sea Beach Rd is a pleasant airy place on the 1st floor. The service and the local food are both good, meals cost Tk 12 to 16.

Opposite the Motel Upal and on the same side of the road as the Hotel Shaibal the *Sagarika Restaurant* has meals for Tk 35.

Getting There & Away

Air There are four flights weekly from Dacca, Tk 450 one-way, Tk 900 return. These same flights can be picked up from Chittagong. Seats are limited and should be booked well in advance. There are twice weekly flights to Chittagong for Tk 145. The Biman office is in the Sayeman Hotel in Room 4 (tel 61-219).

River Launches leave for Cox's Bazar from the Saddarghat in Chittagong on a private basis. The price is negotiable. BIWTC seatrucks operate twice weekly with a fare of Tk 14.

Road There are daily buses from Chittagong. Buses and minibuses to Chittagong and Teknaf leave from 6 am till 3 pm. To Teknaf BRTC buses take three hours and cost Tk 14, local buses take four hours and cost Tk 13.

The road from Chittagong is paved but narrow and potholed. For the first third distance from Chittagong there are villages but then it's dense jungle with just occasional settlements. Around half distance Hindu and Buddhist temples and a few mosques begin to appear.

The route bypasses Harbang at about the midway point. This is the old Arakan road and apparently has a large Buddhist monastery. South of Harbang is Chiringa, actually a military cantonment, and near here is the village of Chokoriya.

There are now direct BRTC buses from Fulbaria in Dacca to Cox's Bazar with a fare of Tk 86.

Burmese Border The overland route across the Burmese border has been closed since the early 1950s.

Getting Around

Rickshaws cost Tk 2-3 within the town or Tk 15-20 by the hour. Babytaxis cost Tk 5-15 within the town perimeter. Jeeps can be hired from the tourist office for Tk 40 per hour plus Tk 5 per mile. Minibuses cost Tk 60 per hour plus Tk 8 per mile.

Cox's Bazar Beach

AROUND COX'S BAZAR

The beaches south of Cox's Bazar are hedged by a low hill range which starts north of Chittagong after Feni and runs all the way to Teknaf.

Himachari Beach

This beach is reached by bus, then a walk across the village to the beach. They produce a lot of pan leaves here. There are low cliffs and gorges just before the beach. It's very quiet here; cattle and buffaloes appear at sunset, their bells tinkling on their way to the village. There are a few picnic facilities.

Inani Beach

This is considered the world's longest and broadest beach: 180 metres at its narrowest at high-tide and 300 metres at low-tide. There are no tourist facilities here and it's usually deserted.

Ramu

This quiet and secluded village is 14 km north of Cox's Bazar on the Chittagong road and a half km from the main road. It is noted for its Buddhist *kyaungs* (temples), pagodas and a beautiful monastery containing images of Buddha in bronze, silver and gold inlaid with precious and semi-precious stones.

Maheskhali Island

Eight km north-west of Cox's Bazar this hilly island is predominantly Muslim and also has a military cantonment. The 160-year-old Adinath Hindu temple tops a hill. This is an attractive island with an interesting history, good fishing, and especially worth a visit during the festive season of Falgoon (March-April). A launch trip will cost Tk 4 and takes one hour, there are small boats which are cheaper. Wear thongs or old shoes as you may have to slop through the mud on boarding and leaving the boat.

Sonadia Island

Just across the river from Cox's Bazar this island is a birdlife sanctuary for migratory birds – petrels, geese, curlews, snipes, shanks, lapwings, ducks and other waterfowl. The western side of the island is a beach, known for its interesting seashells. There is a small bazar here with seashell crafts. The only problem with Sonadia is that there is no regular launch there, nor does Parjatan offer guided tours, so the only way to get there is to hire a boat from Kastorghat at Tk 300-400 for a daytrip.

St Martin Island

About 10 km south-west of the southern tip of the mainland this small coral island has a population of a few thousand. It's a bit of a tropical paradise: beaches fringed with coconut palms, bountiful marine life. There are plans to develop the island as a tourist resort.

Apparently, a permit is required from the military commander in Cox's Bazar, but it is possible to get there without one; make sure your passport and visa are in order. There is no regular boat service there, it costs about Tk 20 to hire one to make the four-hour trip from Teknaf. There are no hotels.

COX'S BAZAR-TEKNAF

This is a three to four-day trek along the beach, which makes it tempting to camp out along the way but it is advised against, especially if you're alone. Take water-purifying tablets and supplementary food and water.

Day 1 A six-to-eight-hour walk up to a river after Himachari beach. The route is pleasantly interspersed with waterfalls along the cliffs. Distance is 24 km.

Day 2 Trek up to Somapura, about the same distance as the first day. There is a resthouse at Somapura, but it's free to stay in the local school.

Day 3 A similar walk to Silkhali where there is another resthouse, but it is possible to spend the night in Baradail Bazar.

Day 4 About 18 km to Teknaf.

TEKNAF

This small town is located on the southern tip of the narrow strip of land adjoining Burma, 92 km from Cox's Bazar. The Naaf River forms the Bangladesh-Burma border here and a creek from the Naaf separates the flat and elevated portions of the town.

Most of the town is a crowded area of narrow alleys but a new mosque of orthodox Islamic design with a tall minaret towers over the area near the bus station. The main reason for visiting Teknaf would be for St Martin Island which lies 36 km to the west. There are, however, no regular launches from Teknaf.

Places to Stay

The *Arafat Hotel* is walking distance from the bus station to the south on the main street. It's pretty basic with shared bath singles at Tk 10, doubles at Tk 20. The similarly priced *Niribili Hotel* is across the creek near the electricity generator. It's better than the Arafat and although the rooms are very narrow they're clean and have mosquito nets. The *Government Rest House* is a little way out of town on the Cox Bazar road. Prior permission is required to stay here.

The *Hotel Naaf International* is modern and fairly clean with singles/doubles at Tk 25/45. There are good views at sunset from the rooftop but there is no restaurant, the shower water is muddy and the drinking water is brackish.

Places to Eat

Some problems getting a decent meal have been encountered in Teknaf; tourists generally come only for the day, taking the early bus there. Those who stay over night have been known to adopt a fairly spartan diet of biscuits and tea or soft drinks until they return to Cox's Bazar. Food tends to be less than hygienic and far from appealing.

Getting There & Away

The Cox's Bazar-Teknaf road is a continuation of the road from Chittagong – narrow, paved, often bumpy, but quite usable. Soon after Ramu a road to Burma forks off to the east. From here on the scenery is noticeably Buddhist with stupas seen above the trees and women seen more frequently on the roadside.

COMILLA

Situated 114 km south-east of Dacca and 150 km north-west of Chittagong, Comilla is a junction point for east Bangladesh travel, making it easy to reach. Located on the border with the Indian state of Tripura, it has begun to be developed as a commercial centre producing pharmaceutical products. The Academy for Rural Development is also located here.

Because of its proximity to the border, Comilla was one of the entry points used by the Indian army when they invaded the country during the war in 1971. The fighting was particularly bitter here. The main reason for *visiting*, as distinct from

passing through Comilla is the 7th-12th century Buddhist ruins, eight km to the west, at Mainimati.

There are two local festivals, the Raas Hindu and Kathin Chibar Dan Utsab Buddhist festivals, which both occur 10 days into November and are incorporated into a local trade fair.

Places to Stay

Hotel Maraj (tel 5151) at Kandil Park is a new place. Rooms generally have shared bathrooms and singles/doubles cost Tk 25/50. From the Central Bus Station or Lal Gate it costs Tk 3 by rickshaw.

Mosque Minarets, Comilla

Hotel Abedin (tel 6014) is on Station Rd near Lal Gate. The green painted hotel has only rooms with shared bath but it's pretty clean and singles/doubles are Tk 20/45. Breakfast is also available and if you're departing early for Sylhet they'll wake you up. From the Central Bus Station it's just a five minute walk.

Hotel People (Janta Boarding) is not far from the Abedin on Station Rd. The sign outside is only in Bangala and rooms cost Tk 25/40 without bath, Tk 50 for a double with attached bath. The *Parjatan Motel* is located at the Old Ferry Ghat in Daukandi. It has four rooms with attached bath, a car park and restaurant; singles/doubles are Tk 25/40 and it's good for motorists.

Places to Eat

There are no Chinese restaurants here nor any middle level eating places. The only choices are the local food stalls at the Central Bus Terminal or Kandil Park where there is a kebab-nan place near the cinema. Other places are very basic.

Getting There & Away

Road & Rail Transport from Comilla is only by road or rail. The southern bus terminal caters for those heading to Dacca, Feni and Chittagong; the northern one, at Lal Gate, is mainly for those going to Sylhet and other northern centres.

To Dacca buses takes 2½ hours and cost Tk 14. By train the fares are Tk 101 in 1st class, Tk 29 in 2nd, Tk 13 in 3rd.

To Chittagong buses takes 3½ hours and cost Tk 28.50. Trains takes 4½ hours and cost Tk 230 in 1st, Tk 60 in 2nd, Tk 27 in 3rd.

To Sylhet buses take eight hours and costs Tk 42. Trains take eight hours also and cost Tk 128 in 1st, Tk 34 in 2nd, Tk 16 in 3rd.

To Mymensingh you take a bus or train up to Bhairab Bazar to get connections.

MAINIMATI RUINS

Eight km to the west of Comilla lies a range of low hills known as the Mainimati-Lalmai ridge. Famous as an important

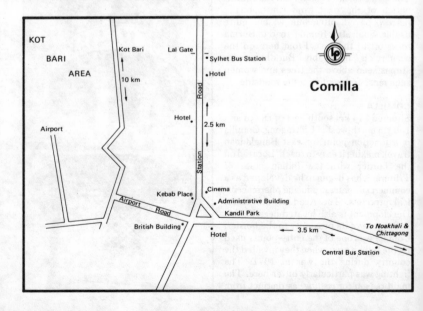

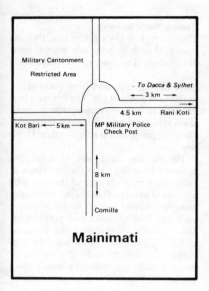

Military Cantonment
Restricted Area

. To Dacca & Sylhet
← 3 km →

4.5 km   Rani Koti

Kot Bari ← 5 km →   MP Military Police
                    Check Post

↑
8 km
↓

Comilla

Mainimati

centre of Buddhist culture from the 7th to 12th century the buildings excavated here were wholly made of baked bricks. There are many scattered archaeological remains here but the three most important are Salban Vihara, Kotila Mura and Charpatra Mura. The whole range of hillocks runs for about 18 km and is studded with more than 50 Buddhist sites. A site-museum houses the archaeological finds excavated here which include terracotta plaques, bronze statues, a bronze casket, coins, jewellery, kitchen utensils, pottery and votive stupas embossed with Buddhist inscriptions.

Mainimati is a military cantonment area in the district of Comilla. It was while the military were clearing the area with bulldozers that the archaeological site in the Kot Bari area was discovered. This was a centre for Buddhism visited by Xuan Zhang in the 7th century AD. The Chinese pilgrim found 70 monasteries, about 2000 bhikkus and an Ashoka stupa of the 2nd century BC.

Salban Vihara

This well-planned 170-metre-square monastery of the Paharpur type has 115 cells for the monks, built around a spacious courtyard with a cruciform temple in the centre facing an elaborate gateway complex. This was discovered during regular excavation in 1957. The royal copper plates of the Deva kings and a terracotta seal bearing a royal inscription which were found here clearly testify that the monastery was built by Sri Bhavadeva, the fourth ruler of the Deva dynasty in the first half of the 8th century. The original cruciform plan of the central temple was changed and reduced in scale during the rebuilding process. The entire basement wall was heavily embellished with terracotta plaques and ornamental bricks, representing the prevailing folk art of the time.

Kotila Mura

Perched on a flattened hillock, five km north of Salban Vihara, the picturesque remains of a unique Buddhist establishment are enclosed within a massive boundary wall. Here three stupas were found during excavations, each representing one part of the Buddhist trinity, or the Three Jewels. Built in the traditional square ground plan with circular drums and hemispherical domes the stupas constitute the Buddha, Dharma and Sangha. The ground plan of the central stupa is in the shape of a 'Dharma Chakra' or the 'Wheel of the Law'. The hub of the wheel or chakra is represented by a deep shaft in the centre and the spoke by eight brick-built cells.

Charpatra Mura

Not far from Kotila Mura is another oblong Buddhist shrine, 55 metres by 16 metres. This was salvaged from the bulldozers of the military in 1958. The main prayer chamber of the shrine is to the west, and approached from a spacious hall to the east through a covered passage. The most important discovery at this site were the four royal copper-plate grants, three belonging to Chandra rulers, the other to Sri Viradhara Deva, a later Hindu king.

Places to Stay

With prior permission from Parjatan in Dacca you can stay in the six room *Archaeological Rest House* where singles are Tk 25.

Getting There

From Kandil Park in Comilla babytaxis run to Kot Bari. The tiny contraptions somehow manage to carry six or seven passengers – the alternative is to hire the whole vehicle for Tk 18 to 21. Rickshaws are more expensive at Tk 35 one-way. Special permission from the District Commissioner is required to take the more direct route from Comilla through the restricted military area.

The site is scattered and difficult to find your way around. Rani Koti, about a half km off the main road and about four km out on the Dacca road, is a good starting point. The building on top of the knoll here marks the centre of the Buddhist site but apart from test lines, said to mark where the walls once stood, there is little to see.

CHANDPUR

Chandpur, a quiet riverport town, offers very little for the traveller in the way of intrinsic attractions. Any point in visiting it will be to use it as a base for exploring the countryside or because it's a good place to travel to or from Dacca by boat.

Places to Stay & Eat

The *Hotel Akbari* on College Rd has singles for Tk 12-25, doubles for Tk 22-35 and is good value. The *Balaka Hotel* in Purana Bazar has rooms with common bath only at Tk 10/20. The *Hotel Safina* on Bagodi Rd is similar in price and standard.

There are a handful of eating places but generally pretty basic and with a very limited choice.

Getting There & Away

Transport from Dacca is by bus, train or launch, though by train one must change at Laksham. The best way is by launch.

River Launches depart from Saddarghat in Dacca at 8 and 11 am. The five hour trip costs Tk 15 with two stops en route, one of them at Munshinganj. From Chandpur for Dacca departures are at 7.30 am and 1.30 pm.

This is the best way of travelling between Chandpur and Dacca. There is fascinating river scenery all the way with all sorts of watercraft to watch – passenger launches, ferries loaded to the rooftops, sailboats with tattered and patched up sails, paddle boats and oar-powered boats. Cargoes vary from sand to vegetables and fruit or sacks of grain. Large country boats are towed by men pulling invisible nylon cord tied to the masts.

Rail There are no direct train services between Dacca and Chandpur – you have to take a very roundabout route. There are four trains daily to Comilla. There are no direct trains to Chittagong, you have to connect at Laksham.

Road From Fulbaria in Dacca there are direct buses to Chandpur or you can take a bus to Comilla and connect from there to Chandpur. As with the train service between Dacca and Chandpur this is a long and rather round-about route.

From Chandpur buses depart every two hours to Comilla. To Chittagong, as with the trains, there is no direct service. You have to changes buses at Feni. To get to Noakhali you must take a babytaxi to Raipur from where buses connect to Noakhali.

SYLHET DISTRICT

Next to the Hill Tracts, Sylhet is the hilliest district in the country. Lying between the Khasi and Jaintia hills to the north and the Tripura hills to the south, the district is essentially one large valley, broken up by innumerable terraced tea gardens, thick tropical forests and large pineapple plantations and orange groves.

Historically, the Sylhet region achieved greatest fame when it was mentioned by Marco Polo as a recruiting centre for eunuchs for the Kingdom of Kamrup. At about this time a great sufi mystic, Sheikh Jallaluddin from Konya, Turkey, came to settle here. Ibn Battuta, a noted Moroccan traveller from Tangier, visited Sylhet to see the sufi – and also picked up a female slave for only Rs 7 while he was there.

The name Sylhet could either have originated from the word *Sri-Hat* – Central Bazar – or from the Arabic term *Serhed* – meaning frontier-town. The district was formerly part of Assam and the north of the district has the highest annual rainfall – 5000 mm (200 inches) – in the country. Just across the border in India is Cherrapunj, the wettest place on earth. On the whole, however, the district has the best climate in the country, temperate, cool with clean, crisp fresh air in winter, just fairly warm in summer.

This is a tea-growing district with more than 150 tea gardens on over 40,000 hectares, producing 30 million kg of tea annually. Tea is Bangladesh's second largest source of foreign exchange – manpower exports to the Middle East are the main source. Sylhet is considered the richest district in the country with its natural resources and agricultural produce which includes oranges, pineapples and mineral resources which include gas reserves and possibly oil deposits. Manufacturing industries include tea processing, cement, urea fertilizer and paper.

The valley is fed by two rivers, the Surma and Kushiara, which wind across the valley floor. In the south the Surma joins with the Meghna. The valley also has a vast number of shallow natural depressions known as *hoars*. These fill with water during the wet season and provide verdant sanctuaries for migratory birds wintering from Siberia. Sylhet's forests are home for leopards, tigers and panthers.

The hilly frontier area at the foot of the Khasi-Jaintia Hills is tribal land. The Khasis, Pangous and the Manipuris who still live here shun regular contact with the outside world, venturing only occasionally from their settlements. The Manipuris are the exception to this, producing craftsmen, jewellers and businessmen who have entered into the general Bangladeshi community. The Manipuri classical dance, seen only during Hindu festivals dedicated to the worship of Radha-Krishna, the consort of Krishna, is the best known feature of Manipuri culture.

The history of the district was principally tribal until the conquest by the Muslims in the 13th century. In the 17th century the Moghul empire overran the region. The Moghuls, who apparently gave the area little importance, gave way in the 18th century to the British East India Company who developed it as part of their Assam tea-growing region.

SYLHET

Though a centre for Muslim pilgrimage during the Tuglukh dynasty, Sylhet was most influenced by the British occupation. They have given this town a unique style of architecture: tall windows shaded by large curved awnings, and roofs topped by several enclosed glass cubicles to provide light and ventilation.

The whole town has a distinctly British atmosphere, more so than other colonial settlements. Apart from the usual administrative buildings, the former residences and social structures seem to have weathered the transition from independence better than many other pieces of British Raj flotsam; colonnaded residences still maintain neatly trimmed lawns, verandahs still have leather armchairs and sofas arranged for delicate tastes. The old clock tower, made entirely of corrugated iron sheeting, also remains although it no longer has a clock. The British Council House on the northern bank of the Surma also remains quaintly picturesque. Sylhet has been referred to as the 'Second

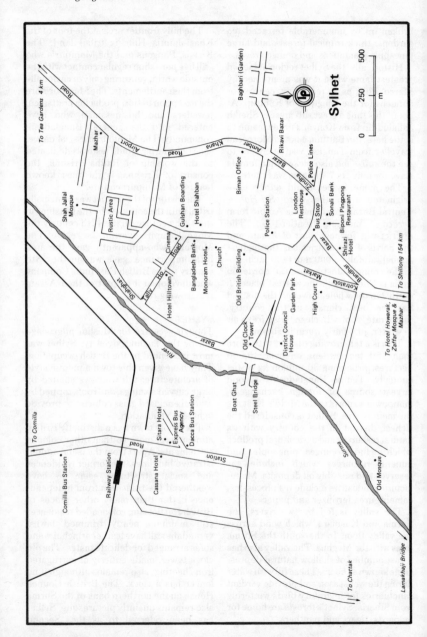

Sylhet

London of Bangladesh'; of the first I am still unsure!

Although not impressive in any spectacular manner, Sylhet has an attractive and pleasant aspect that could easily make it one of the loveliest small cities in Bangladesh. The streets in town are narrow but neatly and cleanly paved. Immediately outside the town are rice paddies, coconut palms and ponds with ducks swimming. To further increase the town's attraction, all points of interest are within walking distance from the town centre.

There a number of mosques of pre-Moghul and Moghul period in and around the town. The medieval Mosque of Sheikh Jallaluddin to the north of the city was recently torn down and replaced by a much larger one with a minaret. To the east of the British Council House on the northern bank of the Surma is a Moghul period mosque enclosed by high walls and topped by a low dome.

The southern region of the town contains the railway station, bus agencies and stations. The buildings of this zone are markedly post-independence in their style and the layout has little sense of order. The Surma River, the local waterway, is traversed by a large steel bridge. It's continually congested with rickshaws, usually pushed by 'assistants' who get paid 50 poisas for the crossing. Because of the bridge there are only a handful of boats ferrying passengers across the river. The railway station, bus stations and bus agencies are on the southern side of the river.

Information

The Sonali Bank in Zindha Bazar exchanges foreign currency. Sylhet has various religious festivals – Muslim, Hindu and Buddhist. The Hindu *melas* are the most colourful – Laspurnima, Jolung Jatra, Rota Jatra – all dedicated to Radha-Krishna. Only during these Hindu melas are the Manipuri dances held.

Things to See

This is a town best seen on foot, not that there is anything of great interest. Try the Lakootola Tea Garden where the manager may lecture you on the history and production of this beverage in exchange for a tour of the factory. The Lakootola and Malinisora tea gardens are about six km from town on the airport road. The tea gardens have scarcely changed in the past century – administration and management remains predominantly British, the workforce mainly Hindu. The river banks are also interesting in a demure fashion, offering a languid view of local lifestyles: fishermen repairing nets, men loading barges.

In the city the shrine of the saint Shah Jallal is of interest; it is visited by innumerable devotees of every caste and creed. The pond next to it is filled with catfish who are, according to legend, the transmogrified descendants of Raja Gour Govinda. For what purpose or crime they suffer this fate we are not told.

On a hillock, named Rama Raja's Tilla, are the ruins of the Palace of Gour Govinda. The ruins of his fort stands near the Murali Chand College.

Places to Stay – bottom end

Hotel Shirazi in Bunder Bazar is fairly basic, singles/doubles with shared bathrooms are Tk 15/30. On Station Rd the *Hotel Sithara* has rooms from Tk 12/20, some with attached bath. The *Hotel Amin* in Bunder Bazar, has a friendly atmosphere although the building is pretty run down. Prices vary from Tk 18 to 30.

The *Parjatan Resthouse*, located in Akbarpur in the tea garden area, has two rooms with a kitchen. They cost Tk 75 per room or Tk 150 for the whole house.

Places to Stay – middle

The *Shahban Hotel* (tel 7459) on Taltola Rd has a restaurant and ordinary rooms for Tk 25/38, aircon and deluxe rooms for Tk 100/200. *Hotel Anurag* (tel 6718) on Dhubadighi North Rd has rooms with attached bath at Tk 25/42, aircon and deluxe rooms for Tk 50 to 200.

The *Gulshan Boarding House* (tel 6437) on Taltola Rd has no English sign. Singles/doubles are Tk 28 but the restaurant has a rather poor selection, there is no coffee and the tea is terrible. The *London Rest House* in Zindha Bazar is a new building with a restaurant which serves local food. Rooms are Tk 25/45. The *Hotel Monoram* on Taltola Rd has rooms with attached bath for Tk 25/50.

Places to Stay – top end
The *Hilltown Hotel* (tel 8262-64) on Tally Ho Rd is the classiest in town. There's a restaurant and bar and singles for Tk 45-50, doubles for Tk 75-85. Rooms with aircon and phone are Tk 200.

Places to Eat
The *Ping-Pong Chinese & English Restaurant* (great name) is on the 1st floor of the Biponi Market Building in Zindha Bazar. There is no sign in English but the cooking is reasonable and the coffee excellent. Curiously it's much easier to get a good cup of coffee in this tea growing centre than a halfway decent cup of tea. The *Hilltown Hotel* on Tally Ho Rd has a restaurant where breakfast is supposed to be pretty good. The *Shahban Hotel* restaurant is also recommended.

Getting There & Away
Air From Dacca Biman has flights three times daily, the fare is Tk 340. The Biman office (tel 6471) is on Shah Jallal Rd in Zindha Bazar.

Rail From Dacca there are two trains daily with fares of Tk 196 in 1st class, Tk 51 in 2nd, Tk 22.50 in 3rd. Departures to Dacca are at 7.30 am and 8.30 pm.

From Comilla there is only one train, the *Chittagong Express*, which takes six to eight hours. 1st class costs Tk 128, 2nd is Tk 34, 3rd Tk 16. To Chittagong there is also only one daily connection – 1st class Tk 230, 2nd Tk 60, 3rd Tk 27. Prior

reservations are necessary for 1st class on any of these routes.

Road Day buses depart Dacca hourly from 6 am to 1 pm. The trip takes 10 hours and costs Tk 55. Express day buses cost Tk 65. Express night buses with VCRs for entertainment cost Tk 70, depart at 8.30 and 9 pm and take just seven hours. The express bus agencies in Sylhet are on Station Rd and Dacca buses depart from here. Departures for BRTC and private ordinary buses are from 7 am. Day express buses depart at 7.30 am, the night express buses at 8.30 pm. Prior reservations are required for the day or night expresses.

From Comilla buses depart from Lal Gate every two hours from 6 am to 1 pm. The trip takes eight hours and there are no express day or night buses between Comilla and Sylhet. Buses for Comilla depart from the Sylhet Bus Terminal on the outskirts of town from 7.30 am.

There are only occasional buses to Chittagong and they also depart early in the morning. There is no direct route to Mymensingh from Sylhet – the route goes via Bhairab Bazar, a road and rail junction where there are connecting buses and trains. Alternatively you can take a bus to Sunamganj via Chattak, then a seven-hour launch trip to Jaysiri, followed by a rickshaw to Chandrabara and from there make a six to seven km walk through pleasant countryside before taking a rickshaw for Mohanganj from where the train fare to Mymensingh is Tk 6 to 10. Sounds very complicated!

AROUND SYLHET
Jaintia
Forty km north of Sylhet, this was the capital of an ancient kingdom which included the Khasi and Jaintia Hills and the Plains of Jaintia. Scattered around this region are a number of ruins which give proof to the level of the kingdom's prosperity.

Madhabkunda

About five km from Kakhinbagh Railway Station there is the famous waterfall of Madhabkunda which attracts a large number of sightseers.

Maulvi Bazar

The district headquarters of Maulvi Bazar stands south of Sylhet on the left bank of the Manu River. There is a beautiful lake, Berry Lake, spread like a horseshoe over an area of about 10 hectares. There is a *Tourist Rest House* here. On the way to Maulvi Bazar is Srimangal, 21 km from Sylhet, where the Tea Research Institute is located.

Other Places

Hakalakhi is reportedly good for bird-watching and angling. Chattak, 38 km north-east of Sylhet, has cement and pulp factories and a sky ropeline used to transport lime from the hills. Fenchuganj is another scenic town, apparently with a wildlife reserve. The hilly and wooded town of Azimganj has tea gardens populated by former expatriates, now affluent businessmen. It is considered the most beautiful town in the whole district of Sylhet.

DACCA-SYLHET

Sylhet is 342 km north-east of Dacca and is linked by what could now properly be described as a highway although stretches may still be unsurfaced. In the open country the scenery is luxuriant, flat, the rice paddies only interrupted by the occasional village. At the Meghna River buses must cross by ferry although there is a rail bridge. The crossing takes half an hour to 45 minutes, running diagonally to the ferry ghat upstream on the other bank. Day buses sometimes make a brief stop in Brahmanbaria although many do not stop at all. Near Brahmanbaria in the village of Sorail, north-east of Ashuganj on the Sylhet-Dacca road, the Sorail Mosque of 1670 has three domes and short towers.

COMILLA-SYLHET

It's 256 km north from Comilla to Sylhet. Unlike the Dacca buses the service from Comilla is a local one with frequent stops and a lengthy pause in Brahmanbaria. Just beyond here there a few old Hindu temples, quite different from those found in India. They are tall and slim with straight lines, tapering off to a sharp point. The yellow of fields of mustard oilseed give way to neatly trimmed tea gardens as you approach Sylhet.

INDIAN BORDER

It used to be that the route to Shillong in India via Tamabil was open to both regional and international traffic, but since the early '70s it has been closed from the Indian side on account of the problems in Assam caused by the influx of illegal immigrants from Bangladesh. Conditions could change in Assam, re-opening the border between Tamabil and Shillong.

It takes three hours to get to Tamabil from Sylhet and a 15-minute hike to the border post, then again 15-minute's walk to Dauki in India, from where buses run to Shillong.

Glossary

Many everyday terms in Bangladesh are exactly the same as in India. This glossary attempts to concentrate more on specifically Bengali words or ones with a particular relevance to Bangladesh.

Al – rectangular elevated area of land found at early settlements in Bengal, probably used as a retreat during floods.

Baksheesh – tip, bribe or simply donation to a beggar.
Bangala (also Bangla) – ancient term for the Bengali people and the land inhabited by them. The name is derived from the bamboo thatch hut with its curvilinear roof design known as a *bang*.

Bazar – market area, a market town is called a bazar.
Bhikkus – Buddhist monks.
Bund – embankment or dyke.

Cantonment – administrative and military area of a British Raj-era town.
Chappati – unleavened Indian bread.
Chowk – courtyard or market place.
Crore – 10 million.

Dacoit – robber, particularly armed robber.
Dhal – lentil soup.

Fakir – a Muslim who has taken a vow of poverty, also applied to Hindu ascetics such as sadhus.
Firman – grant of control of an area of land. Early European trading companies established themselves on the subcontinent by being granted firmans by the Moghuls.

Ghat – steps or landing on a river, the docks for Bangladesh's innumerable ferry services.
Ghee – all purpose cooking oil, clarified butter.

Haji – a Muslim who has made the pilgrimage to Mecca.
Haveli – traditional mansion with interior courtyard.

Idgah – open enclosure to the west of a town where prayers are offered during the Muslim festival of Id.

Jatra – Bengali folk theatre.
Jute – fibre of a plant grown widely in Bangladesh, used to make sacks, mats, etc.

Kabigan – form of folk debate in verse form or poetry.
Khan – Muslim honorific title.

Lakh – 100,000.
Lassi – very refreshing yoghurt and iced water drink.
Longhi – loin cloth wrapped around your thighs.

Mahabharata – Vedic epics, one of the two major Hindu epics.
Masjid – mosque, the Jami Masjid is the Friday Mosque or main mosque.
Mela – festival or fair, usually Hindu.
Moghul – golden period of Indian history from the Emperor Babur to Aurangzeb, the last powerful Moghul ruler.
Monsoon – rainy period when it rains virtually every day.
Muezzin – one who calls Muslims to prayer from the minaret.
Mullah – Muslim priest.

Napi – the decomposed fats of snakes, fish and deer which is considered a delicacy and served during rites and festivals by hill tribes from the Chittagong Hill Tracts.

Pan – betel nut plus the chewing additives.
Parishads – political division of group of villages.

Raga – classical Indian musical composition.
Raj – rule or sovereignty, but specifically applied to the period of British rule in India.
Rajbari – palaces of a small kingdom.
Rickshaw – three-wheeled bicycle-powered vehicle to transport two or more passengers.
Rocket – paddlewheel steamers which operate passenger services around Bangladesh.

Shanti Bahini – 'Peace Army' of the hill tribes in the Chittagong Hill Tracts.
Seer – unit of weight, two lbs.
Subha – province of the Moghul empire.
Sufis – Muslim mystics.

Tari – fermented palm wine, drunk by hill tribes from the Chittagong Hill Tracts.

Thana – village.
Tonga – two-wheeled horse or pony carriage.

Upazila – political division of group of villages.

Varendra – ancient kingdom in what is now Bangladesh. Described in the Mahabharata.

Zamindar – landlord, a Moghul invention where officers were granted a right to land and income from the inhabitants of the land. It was not hereditary and was usually acquired through merit or as a business transaction. The British continued the system for a time before discontinuing it.
Zamindar bari – local governor's residences, rather like the rajbaris of the ancient and medieval periods.

Index

LONELY PLANET NEWSLETTER

We collect an enormous amount of information here at Lonely Planet. Apart from our research we also get a steady stream of letters from people out on the road – some of them are just one line on a postcard, others go on for pages. Plus we always have an ear to the ground for the latest on cheap airfares, new visa regulations, borders opening and closing. A lot of this information goes into our new editions or 'update supplements' in reprints. But we want to make better use of this information so, we also produce a quarterly newsletter packed full of the latest news from out on the road. It appears in January, April, July and October of each year. If you'd like an airmailed copy of the most recent newsletter just send us $7.50 for a years subscription, or for $2 each for single issues. That's US$ in the US or A$ for Australia, write to:

Lonely Planet Publications

PO Box 88, Sth Yarra, VIC., 3141 Australia

     or

Lonely Planet Publications

PO Box 2001A, Berkeley, CA 94702 USA

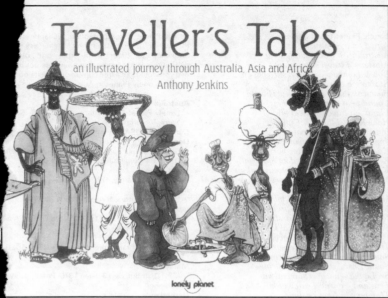

Traveller's Tales

an illustrated journey through Australia, Asia and Africa

Anthony Jenkins

lonely planet

Cartoonist Anthony Jenkins has spent
several years on the road, travelling in
55 countries around the world. Along
the way he has filled numerous sketch-
books with his drawings of the people he
met.

This is a book of people, not places. A
tattooed Iban tribesman in Sarawak, a
mango seller in Cameroon, fellow
travellers in Nepal . . . all are drawn with
perception and (in most cases) affection.

Equally perceptive are Jenkins' written
comments and descriptions of incidents
during his travels. The combined result
is like a series of personal illustrated
letters.

This is a traveller's travel book. If you
have ever endured an Indian train,
watched the world go by in Kathmandu's
Durbar Square or tried to post a letter
in southern Africa, then opening these
pages will be like meeting old friends
and will probably give you itchy feet to
be on the road once more.

Lonely Planet travel guides are available ar
the world. If you can't find them, ask
bookshop to order them from one of
distributors listed below. For countries not li
or if you would like a free copy of our latest bool
write to Lonely Planet in Australia.

Australia
Lonely Planet Publications, PO Box 88, S
Yarra, Victoria 3141.
Canada see USA
Denmark
Scanvik Books aps, Store Kongensgade 59 A
DK-1264 Copenhagen K.
Hong Kong
The Book Society, GPO Box 7804.
India & Nepal
UBS Distributors, 5 Ansari Rd, New Delhi.
Israel
Geographical Tours Ltd, 8 Tverya St, Tel Aviv
63144.
Japan
Intercontinental Marketing Corp, IPO Box 5056
Tokyo 100-31.
Malaysia
MPH Distributors, 13 Jalan 13/6, Petaling Jaya
Selangor.
Netherlands
Nilsson & Lamm bv, Postbus 195, Pampuslaa
212, 1380 AD Weesp.
New Zealand
Roulston Greene Publishing Associates Ltd
Box 33850, Takapuna, Auckland 9.
Pakistan
London Book House, 281/C Tariq Rd, PECHS
Karachi 29, Pakistan
Papua New Guinea see Australia
Singapore
MPH Distributors, 3rd Storey, 601 Sims Drive
#03-21, Singapore 1438
Spain
Altair, Riera Alta 8, Barcelona, 08001.
Sweden
Esselte Kartcentrum AB, Vasagatan 16, S-111
20 Stockholm.
Thailand
Chalermnit, 108 Sukhumvit 53, Bangkok,
10110.
UK
Roger Lascelles, 47 York Rd, Brentford,
Middlesex, TW8 0QP.
USA
Lonely Planet Publications, PO Box 2001A,
Berkeley, CA 94702.
West Germany
Buchvertrieb Gerda Schettler, Postfach 64,
D3415 Hattorf a H.